Maurice H Hervey

The Trade Policy of Imperial Federation From an Economic Point of View

Maurice H Hervey

The Trade Policy of Imperial Federation From an Economic Point of View

ISBN/EAN: 9783744725835

Printed in Europe, USA, Canada, Australia, Japan

Cover: Foto ©Suzi / pixelio.de

More available books at **www.hansebooks.com**

THE TRADE POLICY

OF

IMPERIAL FEDERATION

FROM AN ECONOMIC POINT OF VIEW

BY

MAURICE H. HERVEY

*Principal of Illawarra College, New South Wales; Author of
"Outlines of Political Economy," the "Genesis of Federation," the
"Latest Phase of Imperial Federation," &c., &c.*

LONDON
SWAN SONNENSCHEIN & CO.
NEW YORK: CHARLES SCRIBNER'S SONS
1892

THE TRADE POLICY OF FEDERATION.

AUTHOR'S NOTE.

ENGLAND's Commercial Policy differs so radically from that, not alone of alien nations, but of the component States of her own Empire, that a change, either in her Policy or in theirs, is sooner or later inevitable. Advocates of Protection are just as enthusiastic as advocates of Free Trade; and neither party can see aught of good in the rival system. Others, again, find the solution in Reciprocity or Fair Trade. Now, like most questions in Social Science, Commercial Policy is somewhat intricate; nor is it possible to deal with it intelligently upon other than strictly economic grounds. In the following pages the writer has (in the form of a College Lecture) endeavoured to test the rival systems upon such grounds, and as impartially as possible. With some of the conclusions arrived at, it is possible that the reader will not agree; but it is hoped that he will, at least, be assisted to arrive at conclusions of his own based upon more solid considerations than mere partisan feeling.

M. H. H.

THE TRADE POLICY OF FEDERATION.

SYNOPSIS OF CONTENTS.

PART I.—THE TRADE POLICY OF FEDERATION.

ERRORS of Economists.—Synthesis *v.* Analysis.—Essential Definitions.—The Elements of Production.—Malthus on Population.—Poverty.—Free Trade Economically Contrasted with Protection.—Radical Unsoundness of Protection.—Expediency its only Justification.—Great Britain Productively Compared with the United States. — Why Great Britain adopted Free Trade. — Why the United States adopted Protection.—Which Example should the Colonies follow ?—Considerations upon which their Choice should be Based.—The Penalties of Protection.—Seven chief Factors of National Wealth.—The Question as to how these are affected by the rival Systems exhaustively analysed.—Conditions of future National Polity under which the Colonies might advantageously adhere to Protection. — The Alternative Course.—Britannic Confederation.—Existing Differences of Trade Policy the chief Obstacle thereto.—The essential Bases of Confederation.

THE APPENDIX NOTES.

FAIR TRADE.—Its Inconsistencies.—Its possible Expediency upon a large Scale, and with what Object.

HENRY GEORGE ON FREE TRADE.—A Field for a Hobby-Horse.—The Persistency of Protection well illustrated.—Expediency ignored.

FOREIGN TRADE.—Statistics.—Foreign Trade a subsidiary Item under Protection.—American compared with Colonial Trades.

MANUFACTURES.—Protective Fallacies.—Protective Monopolies of Distribution and Profits.—The Tax upon Consumers.—A Bull-Frog Colony.

EXCHANGE AND CURRENCY.—Exchange defined.—The "Balance of Trade Bugbear."—Exchange tends to Equilibrium.—Examples.—Unreliability of Statistics in Exchange Questions.—Real Tests.—Paper Currency.

PART II.—THE TRADE ECONOMY OF FEDERATION.

COBDENITE Errors.—Unfulfilled Expectations.—Why Foreign Nations are Protectionist. — Expediency. — Protectionist Powers of Endurance.—Reasons.—Why Protection is increasing.—Necessity therefore.—How Great Britain has hitherto evaded Protective Tariffs.—The Sop to Cerberus. —Foreign Trade.—Treaties.—Their Injustice towards the Colonies.—Effects upon British Trade of the Abolition of these Treaties.—The only future Outlet for British Trade. —Britannic Commercial Union.—Should such Commercial Unions be rigidly confined to Communities owing Allegiance to the British Crown?—Proposals for a Britannic Commercial Alliance.—Its Advantages. — Terms upon which Foreign Nations should be admissible.—Estimate of Nations likely to join such Alliance.—British Trade then and now. —Two-thirds of a Loaf better than no Bread.—Prospects of increased Trade.

Basis upon which a Britannic Commercial Union might be formed.—Objections to Free Trade within the Union with Reciprocity towards alien States.—Why the Colonies are Protectionist.—A Compromise essential.

Suggestions for a Basis.—Distinction between staple and secondary Imports.—Great Britain's best Customers.—Her Food Supply analysed.—The "Cheap Loaf."—A cheaper Loaf a near Possibility.—The Sugar-Bounties' Monstrosity. —Other Foreign Bounties.—The Remedy.—Prospective Trade under Commercial Union.—Backward Dependencies. —The Causes.—Estimate of British Trade Twelve Months after Establishment of Union.

Would the Tendency of such a Commercial Union be towards Free Trade or Protection?—The Question examined. — Duration of Protective Tariffs. — The Eight Hours' Question. — Its Influence upon Colonial Trade Policy.—Sketches of Colonial Labour.—Life.—Immigrants.

Financial Effects of a Commercial Union.—The Security now afforded to Investors.—Why Canadian Stocks are preferred to Australian.—Deductions.—Foreign Investments.

Foreign Nations and the Britannic Commercial Union.— Inevitable Consequences upon their Trade.—Great Britain's own Future her paramount Consideration.—The Peace of the World.

Steps towards a Britannic Commercial Union.—Essential Preliminaries.—Efforts already made.—The United Empire Trade League.—Lord Salisbury's Opinion.—Congresses of Chambers of Commerce.—Necessity for an Awakening of Public Opinion.—Conclusion.

PART I.

THE
TRADE POLICY OF FEDERATION.

PROTECTION, FREE TRADE, AND FAIR TRADE.

BY common consent of mankind, the problems of Political Economy have come to be regarded as quite beyond the grasp of ordinary minds; they have been abandoned to the investigations of learned professors who make the "dismal science" their especial province, and the public has impatiently waited for enlightenment. Now, herein, the public intelligence has underrated its own powers, and has overrated the powers of the professors. Philosophy has been trying, for at least a hundred years, to arrive at definite conclusions, and has failed signally. It has steadily adhered to the synthetic instead of to the analytical process of reasoning; it has deposed Bacon, and replaced Aristotle; it has attempted to deduce fact from theory, instead of deducing theory from fact. As the inevitable results, there have been as many different theories as philosophers, who have persistently wasted their energies in upholding their own, or in refuting rival, hypotheses. Each school, convinced of the perfection of its own system, has announced itself prepared to instruct mankind how that perfection may be attained. Mankind, seeing this disagreement among the doctors, has refused to be instructed, preferring to be guided by such glimmerings of truth as experience seems to furnish, or by such notions of expediency as each community individually deems adaptable to itself. Hundred-voiced dogmatic Economy bewails this perverseness, loudly proclaiming that it has established a science upon a basis as firm as the law of gravitation, and quite overlooking the fact that whereas gravitation is a law, acknowledged by all astronomers, which has, in thousands of marvellous ways, proved its truth, the teachings of Political Economy are based (fortunately with a few exceptions) upon theories which, so far from being acknowledged by all Economists, are still the subjects of the fiercest contention, and which, so far from approving their truth in thousands of marvellous ways, need to be bolstered up by thousands of marvellous excuses to account for their practical shortcomings. The bald fact is that the strong modern tendency to reduce all science to hard-and-fast rules has attempted to include a subject which is not a science at all. Science, in its technical sense, means *knowledge* of the laws of Cause and Effect—not theory. Strip Political Economy of the thousand and one theories upon which it is built, and what remains of proven fact?

Not much truly; but that little represents all our knowledge upon the subject. Outside that knowledge it is pure waste of time to wander; upon that knowledge alone are we justified in shaping our course. A common-sense distinction must therefore be laid down between theory and fact upon the very threshold of any inquiry within the domains of this most unscientific of all so-called sciences, whereby much useless discussion will be avoided, the grain sifted from the chaff, and such (unfortunately not very numerous) discoveries as have been made focussed into an intelligible narrative.

THEORY is an assumption of knowledge of the causes which produce known results. To be of any use it must not alone explain the causes of known results in the past, but must be able to predict the future results of (assumedly) known causes. It must in fact be prospective as well as retrospective. When it fulfils these conditions it becomes a fact. If it does not fulfil these conditions, it remains useless—nay, worse than useless, for it chains men's minds to argument instead of inquiry.

FACT is proven, incontrovertible Law of Cause and Effect based either upon perfected theory or upon obvious consequence of action.

Thus, when Ptolemy assumed that sun, moon, and stars revolve round the earth, and, upon this crude hypothesis, founded his system of astronomy, he broached a theory which held its ground for ages, which accounted (after a fashion) for certain apparent natural phenomena, but which could lay no claims to scientific accuracy. When Copernicus assumed the totally opposite hypothesis that the sun is the central star round which all the planets revolve, he too merely broached a theory,—a theory indeed founded upon more intelligent observation than that of Ptolemy, but after all only a theory—liable at any time to be replaced by some other hypothesis. But when Newton brought his giant-intellect to bear upon the rival assumptions and enunciated his "Law of Gravitation," the matter was for ever set at rest: the truth of the Copernican system proved beyond doubt, the absurdity of Ptolemy's suppositions clearly demonstrated. Newton's great law never was a theory; it established its truth at once, and that truth has ever since been confimed by that most convincing of all tests—fulfilled prediction. Newton, indeed, *converted Copernicus' theory into fact*, and established upon a firm basis the most accurate of all sciences, astronomy.

Now, unfortunately, no giant intellect has arisen to do for Political Economy what Newton did for astronomy. The names of Adam Smith and of Stuart Mill are indeed as shining lights to their disciples; but the writings of even these prophets contain a ton of theory to an ounce of fact. The greatest discovery hitherto made came from an obscure parson named Malthus, and *he* did his best to conceal the real value of his wonderful "Law of Population" by plastering it over with silly hypotheses. There would appear to be some irresistible attraction for Economists generally to wander off into abstract speculations. And yet there seems to be no valid reason why anyone, *not* an Economist, should not be able to form tolerably clear ideas upon any given branch of the subject without straying off into the foggy regions of theory. Elementary ideas they necessarily must be, from the very small amount of available information. But inasmuch as the subject of Trade (the special field for inquiry in this essay) is essentially elementary too, we may entertain reasonable hopes of arriving at a few important conclusions based upon something more satisfactory than hypothesis.

There is a venerable story, current in Bar messes, concerning a well-known legal luminary who, when asked his opinion upon a very open case, replied: "I'd take a hundred guineas and argue it either way." Now, if it be easy for a speaker to argue an open question either *pro* or *con*, it is very much easier for a writer to do so. He has merely to follow the lazy example of the times: procure some well-known work written in favour of the side he means to attack, and some other standard work upon his own side; this provision gives him a cut-and-dried plan to work upon. By a judicious admixture in his own composition, of criticism of the one, echo of the other, occasional original interjections about national prosperity, waves of depression, and other safe ambiguities, copious statistical lists, etc., he can, if he be a ready writer, rattle off "copy" to any required extent, and take definite rank in the dismal army. The objection to this simple plan is that it never leads to any result. The new work, in its turn, becomes the groundwork for some other writer to operate upon. Criticisms are re-criticised, echoes are re-echoed, fresh and more high-sounding ambiguities are introduced, and more recent statistics are copied out. Thus the game goes on in a circle. No one is convinced. No one, except (possibly) the authors and their publishers, derives any benefit. The scheme of this lecture, whatever may be its defects in execution, is, at least, laid upon different lines. I hold that no individual mind should assume to dogmatise upon a question of national polity which it is within the province of the national legislature alone to decide. The cause neither of Free Trade nor of Protection will ever be won by vociferous denunciation, by authoritative assertion, or by wearisome reiteration of stock arguments. The legitimate object of inquiry *is* to inquire, not to preach; to place clearly before the community the full meaning of the alternatives between which that community has to choose, not to dictate the choice.

Now, if the question could be decided by the standard of right and wrong, Free Trade would at once emerge triumphant. All restraint placed upon naturally-legitimate freedom of action is very obviously an infringement of natural right. Protection is such a restraint, and therefore *naturally* wrong. But so also are Customs-duties, so also are hundreds of regulations tolerated in all civilised communities. Natural right and civilisation cannot exist side by side. The only standard recognised by civilised man is expediency; and it is by this standard that naturally-right Free Trade and naturally-wrong Protection must be judged. This makes a wonderful difference. Protection, which before had not a leg to stand on, can now show a very good leg indeed. It now becomes necessary to decide, *under what conditions (if any) may radically-wrong Protection be advantageously substituted for radically-right Free Trade?* This sounds very paradoxical; but it is the main issue. Ben Jonson laughed at Shakespeare for writing—

"Know, Cæsar doth no wrong but with just cause!"

And Shakespeare, yielding to the criticism, altered

the line. He might have allowed the seeming paradox to stand. *Summum Jus, summa injuria.*

Unsatisfactory as I hold the system followed by the theorists to be, I very willingly concede the convenience of employing the terms used by them; with this important limitation, however, that clear, definite, consistent meanings be attached to these terms. Economic philosophers fight like cats over the words used in a definition, each one striving to mould it in exact accordance with his particular hobby; whole chapters are devoted to this word-torturing. One great prophet, Ricardo, made the startling discovery that unused land is unprofitable or, as he put it, triumphantly, at the end of a voluminous treatise, " land newly brought into cultivation pays no rent for the first year," and insisted on embodying his inspiration in any accepted definition of rent. This proposition threw the Economic philosophers into a frenzy of excitement seventy years ago, and is still awaiting final judgment. Rent fortunately is outside our present limits; but a great many other equally unsettled terms are not, and must forthwith be stated in the language of common-sense.

PRODUCTION: the conversion of a valueless substance into a valuable commodity; or of potential, into actual, value.

CAPITAL: the saved surplus of past, and one of the essentials to future production; the portion of wealth devoted to production.

PROFITS: the additional value of, or increment to, capital after production.

WAGES: the present wealth of labour; the share of labour in profits of production discounted by capital.

WEALTH: *(actual)* the whole amount possessed of the results of production; *(potential)* the undeveloped sources of production.

POVERTY: the manifestation of the inadequacy of wages to support those dependent upon labour.

DISTRIBUTION: the direction of the agencies of production, or of the results of production, into the most profitable channels.

TRADE: the exchange of valuable commodities for other valuable commodities or the equivalent.

FREE TRADE: unrestricted international Trade.

FAIR TRADE: proposal to conduct commercial dealings upon principles of reciprocity.

PROTECTION: restricted international Trade.

DISTRIBUTION OF LAND: devoting land to that particular branch of production for which it is by nature best suited.

DISTRIBUTION OF LABOUR: equivalent to what is generally termed "division of labour;" that is continuously employing the same labour upon the same branch of production.

DISTRIBUTION OF CAPITAL: judicious investment of capital in the most profitable branches of production.

EXCHANGE: technical Trade term including all means adopted of obviating necessity for transmitting specie.

CURRENCY: ordinary coinage, etc., in local circulation.

There are three essential elements to production: land, labour, and capital. This is merely briefly expressing the obvious facts that all produce comes directly or indirectly from the land, that labour is necessary to obtain this produce, and that capital is required to assist labour in its task. These elements may with great exactness be likened to three horses of different degrees of speed harnessed to the chariot of production. The pace at which this chariot can travel will also be the pace of the slowest horse in the team. This is Land, which can only be induced by the most strenuous efforts of the other two to quicken his naturally slow gait; *he* is the only check (but a very effectual one) upon *their* otherwise incalculable speed. Capital is a quiet animal enough (by Foresight, out of Thrift), willing and able to keep up with Labour if only Land would let him. Labour is a wilful, headstrong racer (by Devil-may-care, out of Improvidence), continually injuring himself by his wild struggles to forge ahead. In all seriousness, the limited capabilities of land, both from its absolutely unalterable extent and its slow capacity for improvement, are at the bottom of all human race troubles. And although the amount of available land is eternally fixed, yet but a small fraction of it is actually turned to the best advantage; nay, the productivity of even that small fraction may, by practical research, be vastly increased. Surely no nobler field for philanthropic effort exists. He who brings but an acre of hitherto waste land into cultivation has done a God-like action; he has practically created, if not life, the means whereby life is sustained. God speed the pioneer! he is the true Economist, though he never heard of the "wealth of nations."

Of the very utmost importance also is the proper distribution of land. The next best thing to rendering unproductive land productive is evidently to make the best use of land already available; and that policy is equally evidently to be commended which assists distribution. The rival claims of Free Trade and Protection upon this point will very shortly be shown.

The definition already given of capital sufficiently

explains both its nature and its functions. It must neither be confounded with wealth, of which it is only a component part, nor with money, which is but one of the numerous forms under which it appears.

Labour is the most unmanageable of the three elements, not from man's ignorance of its nature, but from the fact that it runs counter to man's own nature. The one solid fact so far evolved from the *nebulæ* of economic philosophy, is contained in Malthus' "Law of Population," to which reference has already been made; and that law is the Nemesis of labour. Shorn of theoretical embellishments, it may thus be expressed: "*Population tends to increase very much faster than the means of subsistence.*" Malthus tried to reduce it to mathematical accuracy by actually defining the several rates at which population and production tend to increase; the former he affirmed follows a geometrical, and the latter an arithmetical ratio, *i.e.* population tends to increase as the figures 1, 2, 4, 8, 16, etc., production as the figures 1, 2, 3, 4, 5, etc. He furthermore attempted to show that a given population would, if unchecked, double itself in 25 years, and would, if still unchecked, repeat the doubling indefinitely. To give him his due, he made out a very strong case both for his ratios and for his doubling period. But he proved neither. The sum-total of his arguments, backed by such historical experience as he could discover, by no means entitle his figures to rank as part and parcel of the law itself. He would have acted more wisely had he omitted them; but that could hardly be expected of a theorist. As a result of his over-anxiety for mathematical accuracy, he left himself open to a storm of criticism which has blinded men's eyes to the real value of his enunciation. His numerous opponents naturally attacked him on his weakest points, and by throwing discredit upon his figures, threw discredit also upon his law, of which, in reality, these figures were an unnecessary, ill-judged, attempted illustration.

The intrinsic truth of the law itself is obvious; it is confirmed by the history of the past, fully justified by the convincing experience of the present, and (so long at least as human nature shall remain unchanged) an unerring index to the future. To any one who shall calmly consider it, it is a terrible law, from which there is no escape. Its conclusions are grim and inevitable. No more persons can exist than there is a supply of necessaries to support. That supply cannot be increased, with all our efforts, as fast as these persons can multiply without any effort at all. Those for whom there exists no provision must die of want if they are born. Neither the " struggle for existence " nor the " survival of the fittest," are empty sounds; they are hard, everyday realities.

This ineradicable tendency of population to outrun production is obviously the cause of poverty; and poverty, in its turn, is the great drag upon labour. A labourer's wages include his share in the profits of production as well as providing him with the means of subsistence; they should therefore be more than enough for his support. So they are. In no civilised community do a man's wages only just suffice for his own livelihood. There is always a surplus, small or great; and upon that surplus those dependent upon the labourer have to rely for the means of existence. For how many such dependents will this surplus be sufficient? The answer to this question will, of course, vary in different localities and at different times. Is it possible to strike an average? It is, by comparing the wages paid to any particular class of labourers including or excluding their maintenance; or, in other words, by observing the difference in wages received by labourers who, as they term it, "find themselves" and by those who are "found" by the employer. It will then appear that, taking a general average of all descriptions of unskilled labour, very nearly two-thirds of the labourer's earnings are consumed by himself, leaving, consequently, a little over one-third for the support of those dependent on him. In skilled labour, these proportions vary materially; it costs, for instance, no more to feed a bricklayer than it does to feed a hodman, and the difference in rate of wages tells heavily in favour of the bricklayer's surplus. The disproportion is still more marked when we come to consider what may be termed scientific labour (the professions, art, brain work generally). It is therefore easily understood that a doctor or a mechanic can contrive to support a wife and family; but how can the tens of thousands of unskilled labourers do the same? Does it not simply become a struggle to feed perhaps half-a-dozen mouths with food insufficient for two, to say nothing of shelter and clothing? Is it not a prolonged series of experiments to prove the very smallest amount of necessaries upon which life can be sustained? And do not the subjects of the experiments die off in shoals? Poverty, the most terribly expressive word in the language, simply embodies the natural sequence of effect from cause.

Unfortunately, mankind will not see this, or, at all events, will not act as if it saw it, preferring any explanation offered to the right one. The Economists for once are not to blame; they are, upon the whole, sane enough on this point. But other theories are eagerly pushed forward: Socialist-theories, Radical-theories, Ranter-theories, theories of every degree and shade of logical absurdity. We are urged to confiscate all property and re-divide it fairly. Would that increase the amount of the property? We are warned to remove class distinctions. Would that put the yokel upon a level with the man of science? We are told from the pulpit that poverty springs from human wickedness. Is that consistent with the teachings of Him who foretold that "the poor ye shall always have with you"? I have said that the Economists see this particular matter in the right light, so far as cause and effect are concerned. But they break out as wildly as ever as soon as they leave fact and attempt to show how the evil may be mitigated. Malthus, followed by a numerous clerical school, advocates what he calls moral restraint, that is, that human beings should not breed so fast. This is not bad advice—theoretically. Practically it weighs as nothing against the very strongest of all human passions; nay, the clergy themselves are proverbially the worst offenders. Other philosophers advocate emigration, omitting, however, to indicate how such wholesale depopulations, as alone could produce any marked effect, are to be carried out, or how, even if that difficulty could be got over, the emigrants are to live during the period when, as Ricardo has it, new land "pays no rent." A third school bids us not to trouble ourselves at all upon the subject. Starvation, with its train of diseases, murders, etc., is, we are informed, a natural and infallible "check to overpopulation." Wars, too, we learn, help largely; whilst baby-farms, though doubtless very shocking to humanitarian principles, were, until stopped, of great economic value. Statistics would tend to show that society has tacitly adopted the cold-blooded views of this third school. In Europe, the poor swarm; famine is chronic; disease is daily assuming fresh forms; the hangman still earns a living; ten millions of armed men are ready at a word to butcher one another; infanticide keeps the coroners busy. Can nothing be done? Are all nations, however seemingly prosperous their present condition, doomed to culminate in *this*? If they follow in the beaten track of older nations—yes; what can save them? If they base their social polity upon the lines plainly indicated by experience, by common sense, and by the simple considerations of profit and loss—no; evil results cannot follow from good policy. New countries, young communities, enjoy enormous advantages. Production is so easy that it can for a time defy population; nay, in its exuberance, it challenges and invites population, just as if that all-devouring monster would not come quite soon enough of his own accord. "More labour!" is the cry. "The country must be developed, and then we'll be a great nation." So long as production keeps well ahead, or, at least, well abreast of population, this national enthusiasm to "grow up" quickly is a charming thing to contemplate. There never was a child yet who did not sigh for maturity; but how many struggling men and women sigh for childhood again? What has the well-fed, well-paid labourer living in a small community to gain by that community's growth? Does he suppose his wages will be greater? Does his brother-yokel in thickly-peopled England or France or Germany enjoy greater profits than he Or is it a more glorious thing to be a unit of thirty millions than a unit of half a million? What *is* the cause of this intense longing for a big census? Whatever it be, it is a worthless one. National prosperity, *i.e.* the comfortable existence of all classes of the community, is *not* synonymous with national wealth. England possesses more national wealth than Holland, ten times more perhaps. But can she be compared in point of prosperity of her people to that glorious little country which has not a pauper within its boundaries? The Dutch are not a brilliant nation, they lack the "go-ahead" qualities upon the possession of which the Anglo-Saxon so much prides himself; but they have a truer conception of material welfare than any other people in the world; they realise—they show by their laws, by their customs, by their systems, that they realise the full benefits of rational distribution of the elements of production. Their territory is small; much of it has been recovered from the ocean; every year sees many thousands of acres of hitherto water-covered soil added to the national estate; their engineers are now draining the Zuyder Zee into a new province. This is going at the root of the social problem with a vengeance! The Dutch have a most unfavourable climate, but they make the most of it. They have learnt by experience what they can produce best, and in their own lines of produce they stand unrivalled. *What they cannot produce at a minimum cost, they buy*—the very essence of commercial wisdom. Among the dense native populations of even Java and Mandura, they have introduced the distributive "culture system," which abundantly supplies all local wants and leaves a large margin of produce for exportation. Finally, they have strict, somewhat repressive, laws on the subject of marriage, and a very pronounced public opinion against undue procreation. Other nations, with singular unanimity, select the Dutch as typically slow and dull. These are not such bad qualities in the race which ends in the goal called Poverty. *Festina lente* is good advice to nations, as to individuals. Be it never forgotten that labour *alone* is not a source of wealth, that it only becomes a source of wealth when it acts in harmony with the two other elements of production. To be thus in harmony, it must not exceed their requirements, and it must be divided so as to meet these requirements; it must, in short, *neither exceed the demand nor be unevenly distributed.* If these two conditions could be realised, an ideal state of society would follow; but, unfortunately, the first is practically past hoping for, so long as

Man on many multiplies his Kind.

The second condition it should be the main object of national polity to fulfil.

Now it is worthy of notice that whereas the value of distribution of labour (or "division of labour" as it is often called) is pretty generally appreciated in particular instances, its application to large bodies of men is rarely dwelt upon; while the corresponding importance of an intelligent general distribution (we use the word throughout in the sense already defined) of land and capital is left entirely to individual enterprise. It is assumed that mankind will, without teaching, naturally devote land to that form of production to which it may be best suited; that capital will follow suit because it tends to seek the most profitable investment; and that labour must follow land and capital. People are neither such fools, it is urged, as to attempt to grow sugar-cane in Canada, nor to neglect the opportunity of profitably employing capital in New Guinea. This style of argument simply begs the whole question. It assumes a generally-diffused knowledge amongst mankind of the various capabilities of different localities, whereas in point of fact few men know anything of the nature of even the soil they dwell upon. The common question is, *not*, "What will this ground grow best?" but, "What do I want it to grow?" The general ignorance of even the most elementary geological indications is still more marked.

How many men have starved upon apparently barren soil which contained mines of mineral wealth a few feet from the surface? It is surely but feeble argument to credit men with powers of selection and discrimination which their utter ignorance debars them from possessing. Legislation has simply been stagnant upon questions which should be the subjects of nine-tenths of all statesmanship; the so-called departments of agriculture, mining, geological survey, etc., are but a mere instalment of urgently-needed activity.

In view of the subject of the present work, we are now prepared to estimate the relative merits of Free Trade and Protection from the all-important standpoints of production and distribution; their bearings upon international relations will more conveniently be considered later on. For the moment, the most evident fact is that the better policy is that which most encourages rational distribution and, necessarily, also production. Now, which will the more tend in this direction: a policy which restrains men's liberty of choice, or a policy which leaves that choice free? Obviously the latter. Which then is the restraining policy and which the free? The very names of the rival systems sufficiently foreshadow the answer; but names are sometimes misleading and require to be dissected.

The whole idea of Free Trade is based upon the belief that every man is the best judge of what will be to his own advantage; and that, hence, the community, as a whole, will gain most by non-interference with legitimate individual freedom of action. This view would certainly appear to allow mankind to exercise to the fullest extent such small powers of judgment as the prevalent ignorance, already bewailed, admits of. No man will, for instance, attempt to produce a commodity which he cannot afterwards dispose of at a profit. He will naturally devote his energies to that particular branch of production wherein he enjoys some special advantage of climate, soil, situation, etc. Like our slow-moving Dutch kinsmen, what he cannot profitably produce, he will buy. And, assuming him to have correctly estimated his own best-paying line, he will be in the enviable position of producing at a minimum of cost, of selling, therefore, at a maximum of profit, and of being able to purchase necessaries, which he could not himself produce except at a loss, at their market value. More than this cannot surely be expected; what more, indeed, *could* be attained, unless products rained down from heaven as did the manna of old? It is quite beside the question to object that men do not, under Free Trade principles, secure all these benefits. That is not the fault of the principles but of men's as yet dense ignorance of the particular capabilities of different sorts of land under different conditions of climate and situation; and also the fault of those communities which, by refusing to recognise the principles, block a large portion of the markets of the world. The Free Trade community has, at least, the comfort of knowing that its production will increase in natural, enduring channels with the gradual spread of knowledge upon the subject of distribution.

Protection is an attempt to substitute artificial for natural laws of production. So far we have no quarrel with it; the vast majority of human ordinances are artificial, and where it can be shown that they are an improvement upon natural laws, they should unhesitatingly be adopted. Is Protection such an improvement? How does it look from a productive or from a distributive point of view? Well, at the first glance, Protection does not favour *profitable* distribution, though it encourages, or tries to encourage, every known form of production. This is a very sweeping charge, but very easily proved. Protection aims at self-support, at commercial independence of foreign products. It begins by refusing to admit foreign manufacturers to compete with its own, and calls this "encouraging native industry." But native industry must have raw material to work upon, and, of course, wants to get its material at Free Trade prices. To this the native producers object, refusing to see why they should sell, say, hides at Free Trade price and buy boots at Protection price. They, therefore, must be protected too. Then other industries must be protected.

Finally, everybody and everything is protected. For a time all things look flourishing; business is brisk, lots of money circulate, and everyone is content. Then comes Nemesis with slow, unerring steps into the fool's paradise. Things begin to look gloomy; business is slack, money is scarce, everyone is grumbling. What has happened? A "wave of depression!" cry Protectionists, "which, sweeping over the world, has even affected *us* for the moment!"

Waves of moonshine! What have waves of *anything* to do with a community which deliberately shuts itself out from the commercial sisterhood of nations? If this be so, then Protection does *not* mean commercial independence—has not even that shadowy claim to be respected. What then really *has* happened? Nothing, except an inevitable sequence of effect after cause. While Protection throve, this is what was going on: an enormous and varied assortment of production was engaged in; it was only necessary to get any article added to the Protective tariff to make it at once a profitable line—for local consumption; and capital flowed in freely. These were the halcyon days, before the local supply overtook the local demand. Every one, it is true, paid dearly for everything; but what did this matter when wages were high and work plentiful? The producers of raw material did not mind paying Protection rates for manufactured articles, because they were getting Protection prices for *most* of their produce, and could ship the surplus to Free Trade markets. The manufacturers were simply scratching one another's backs. The working-men, as is usual with the class, reckoned their earnings rather by the number of shillings *per diem* than by the purchasing power of those shillings. Working-men from other communities, likewise confusing number with value, flocked in, thereby taking "some of the gilt off the gingerbread," however. The national legislators rubbed their hands and pointed to the flourishing results of Protection. In their eyes, from their mouths, the position was clear. The country was exporting its surplus produce: this was clear gain. The country was *not* importing foreign produce: this was clear avoidance of loss. It was all (or nearly all) *get* and no *give*. It seems strange that this very one-sidedness has never raised doubts as to the soundness of Protection. It is on record that an eccentric person once exposed real sovereigns for sale, at one shilling each, in a crowded London street, for many hours, *without finding a single purchaser*. It is not easily credible that any one will deliberately trade at a loss; if he appears to do so, there is usually "something behind."

Now if Protection be sound and have *really* this enormous *apparent* advantage in its dealings with Free Trade, there can be nothing in store for the latter but bankruptcy; every year Protection *must* go ahead, and every year Free Trade *must* go astern. Alas for theory! there *is* something behind, a very big something, a very awkward something to get round, a something called over-production. We have glanced at Protection in its glory; let us observe it under a cloud. Much-encouraged production helped on by rash, beguiled, over-sanguine distribution, has gone well ahead of all local demand. Now mark the contrast. The producer, instead of being able to sell *most* of his produce at Protection rates, and export only an inconsiderable portion of it, now finds the local market glutted, and is driven either to sell at home at unremunerative rates, or keep his produce on hand, or export it to Free Trade markets. Very nice alternatives. If he sells at home, he loses; if he does not sell at all, he loses; if he exports, he—let us see how he fares if he exports. The produce he has to sell has been *produced at Protection rates*. If he exports, therefore, he has to compete against produce raised at Free Trade rates in a Free Trade market; and that means dead loss. Whether he be raw producer or manufacturer matters only in degree; lose he must. The working-man sees the number of his shillings *per diem* steadily diminishing, and has become so much accustomed to paying Protection prices that he is slow to realise their additional purchasing power in a glutted market. He grumbles, gets up mass meetings, and clamours for more Protection—meaning, of course, more shillings. Legislators make the most of waves of depression, talk loudly of retrenchment and economy, clap on a few more items to the tariff, and look eagerly round for a " scape-goat "—bloated millionaires and big estates are always available at a pinch. But, henceforth, Protection is playing a losing game. In a rich community, with vast natural resources to fall back upon, it is possible for it to die very hard. Certain classes of producers, manufacturers, and working-men may thrive throughout the piece. Vested interests, based on Protection, will nail their colours to the mast and fight to the bitter end rather than throw open the closed ports on which they have relied. A sudden reversion of the national policy would inevitably mean equally sudden ruin to many. Perhaps the very worst features in the Protection system are, its fascination over men's minds even after disaster, and the extreme difficulty of at once rescinding it without serious immediate national loss. Like all other errors, it must sooner or later be atoned for. But there would seem to be no reason why the atonement should not be gradually effected, why a mistaken policy (once recognised) should not be gently replaced by a sound one without seriously disorganising society.

You cannot without much reflection realise the difficulty of instituting comparison between the rival systems, with respect to different branches of commercial polity, without intermingling these branches. Thus, in dealing with production, I have purposely refrained, so far as possible, from all direct reference to foreign trade, because this latter is reserved for separate and special analysis. I therefore deprecate the numerous objections which might be advanced did our inquiry end here, premising that I will, before we take leave of the subject, anticipate, and (to the best of my power) answer, most of these objections.

Consumption is the using-up of the fruits of production; it is obviously as necessary to human welfare as production itself, of which, indeed, it is the natural consequence. It is a bad thing for production to lag behind consumption, because that means want. But it is also a bad thing for consumption to lag behind production, because that means stagnation. Here we get a sample specimen of theoretical humbug. From the days of Adam Smith it has been "an accepted theory" that consumption of all things not necessary to human existence is destructive to national growth, that (to quote the stock example invariably trotted out) "the spend-thrift is a greater public enemy than the miser," because, as is alleged, capital expended upon champagne and cigars is "wasted," which might have been devoted to cheese and mangold-wurzel, whereas a miser's capital is simply temporarily withdrawn from active service. Heavens! to what lengths will not theorists go! Let us suppose that all civilised men followed up this precept and hoarded up all capital not required for production of necessaries. Result? Extreme cheapness and abundance of necessaries? Not a bit of it. Every one being intent on saving, consumption would be at a minimum, production would be at a minimum too, and enforced idleness would follow. Mankind would simply relapse into the indolent stagnation of savage life—if such existence can be called life. Consumption is the index to production. The greater the consumption, the greater the production tends to be. The greater the production, the greater the distribution. The greater the distribution (most important of all), the greater the general welfare. So long as enough of a nation's capital is devoted to the necessary production required to meet necessary consumption, the residue is better employed ministering to human enjoyment and happiness (not synonymous with bare food, raiment, and shelter), than in lying idle, the whole Army of Faddists to the contrary notwithstanding. Luxury consumption becomes an evil only when it encroaches on necessary capital. The mediæval baron who threw away the year's savings of a thousand peasants upon a suit of gilt armour was an unmitigated curse to the community, because there was no surplus capital to replace his pillage. The modern baron who spends a portion of his rents in carriages, and horses, and pictures, and wines, furnishes employment to carriage-builders, and horse-breeders, and artists, and wine-growers. His rents are not required for necessary production. They belong to the vast surplus capital of the nation. Experience has taught the community that they so belong, and that they will *not* be devoted to necessaries alone. The community takes its measures accordingly, and some of its members engage in the branches of production shown, by experience also, to be what they *will* be devoted to. To sum up, the capital of the community is greater than can be profitably employed in necessary production; surplus capital will *not* engage in production, the results of which must either be given away or allowed to rot; therefore, it *must* either be locked up or be devoted to supply the demands of luxury consumption. Adam Smith and Franklin, upon consumption, always suggest two questions: Did they ever drink wine, or smoke, or use a carriage? Did they ever read More's *Utopia*?

If now we proceed to compare our rival systems from a consumption point of view, we shall find ourselves going over much of the ground already traversed in dealing with production. One point, however, becomes more strongly emphasised. Protection, which aims at supplying all the demands of its own local consumption, can only do so within certain limits, always at a heavy, and often at a prohibitive cost.

C

No more effective restraint upon consumption could well be devised, without a revival of the "old sumptuary laws." If a man has to pay double prices for the articles he consumes, he will certainly not consume so largely as he otherwise would. And if (as but too often follows from a Jack-of-all-trades system) the double priced article is of inferior quality besides, he will, if he possibly can, dispense with it altogether. And if, owing to a deficiency in the local supply, a commodity has to be imported, that commodity will, almost to a certainty, be inferior, since it has to come to the market saddled with a Protective duty. Both foreign manufacturers and local middlemen know very well that this duty added to the cost of a superior article would make the latter too dear to be saleable. Ready sale is all they look to; the Protective duty comes out of the consumer's pocket, not out of theirs; the inferior article is imported, and the unhappy consumer finally gets neither fair value nor fair quality. Herein neither the manufacturer nor the middleman is to blame; each simply adopts the only course consistent with Protection and his own profit. It is the consumer who controls legislation; if he suffers, he may thank his own stupidity.

From even this brief analysis of the effects of Protection upon local production and distribution, it will be seen that it is, as I foreshadowed, *radically* an unsound system; and the more exhaustively you think the matter out, the more strikingly will this *radical* unsoundness appear. But, as also previously intimated, this does not definitely decide the question at issue. It could just as easily be shown that standing armies are radically a mistake, an impoverishing drain upon the resources of a nation. Yet standing armies, as the world is at present constituted, are, from motives of expediency, not alone justifiable but necessary. No doubt in the days of the millennium they will cease to be required. But in the meanwhile it would be very ruinous policy for, say, England to disarm and oppose common-sense logic to Russian ironclads; she would infallibly get the worst of it practically, however sound her peaceful principles might theoretically be. She maintains forces by land and by sea not because it is a morally proper thing to do, but because it is expedient, because it *pays*, because it would *not* pay to disband them. Other nations shape their policy upon similar lines; and, with a fervour as ludicrous as it is impious, each invokes the God of peace to bless the weapons of war. Now national armaments are but measures of Protection designed to secure national interests. We are not playing upon the word. Armies and fleets are but warlike expressions of the same idea as that embodied in peaceful duty-tariffs: both seek to protect a community from being victimised by other communities; the adoption of either, or of both, *may* be justified by necessity or expediency; and of such necessity or expediency each community will judge for itself, unrestrained by moral, logical, or any other theoretical considerations. It is therefore *not enough* to demonstrate that a given policy, such as Protection, is unsound in principle. It is necessary, indeed, to do so in order to make out a *prima facie* case against it; and such a case we have endeavoured to state. But when that is done, it must further be brought home to Protectionist, or would-be Protectionist, communities that Protection is also inexpedient and unnecessary. If this be not done, nothing is done: the Protectionists simply shrug their shoulders and say, " Protection may be as bad as, or even worse than, you describe it ; it may be radically as rotten as sin, but *it suits our book!* " Wherein the Protectionists display considerable judgment, for possible EXPEDIENCY is the one solitary leg their system has to stand upon. That Protection *may* be adopted with success they invariably seek to prove by pointing to the marvellous growth of the United States, nor do Free Traders at all weaken this illustration by quoting the Trade returns of England. Both nations have grown enormously wealthy by pursuing totally different systems ; but this fact would tend rather to prove that *both* systems may be, under different conditions, politic, than that one is inferior to the other at all times and in all places. And that this is in reality a correct inference may conclusively be established by an unbiassed comparison of the great rivals.

In one element of production England is definitely and irremediably deficient—extent of land. She is limited to an area, including Wales, Scotland, and Ireland, of 121,000 square miles; and she is not especially favoured in the matter of climate. A century ago she was already rich in the two other elements, labour and capital. She was moreover what would now be called Ultra-Protectionist; she not only kept foreign products out of her markets by a perfectly crushing tariff, but she taxed even her own products, if exported. Corn, for instance, was taxed both ways to famine prices. She tried to force her Protectionist policy upon the North American Colonies, and lost them in the attempt. But she adhered to her exclusive doctrines at home with unswerving fidelity, until the popular objection to starve upon Protected corn culminated in an outburst, under Richard Cobden, which sounded the knell of Protection in England. A very remarkable man was this same Richard Cobden; a man who, with little pretension to education or culture, saw the errors of the prevalent system in a light which scholarly statesmanship had no glimpses of. "Bread," he argued, "is of paramount importance to the community; and therefore a policy which tends to make bread scarce and dear must be rotten." This was the burthen of his cry from his place in Parliament. Time after time the Protectionist House threw out his bills. Time after time he returned to the charge. At last the force of his argument came home to Sir Robert Peel, and that clear-headed minister succeeded in passing bills, in 1842-46, which practically established Free Trade in corn. This was the thin edge of the wedge which, now thoroughly aroused, public opinion soon drove home. England, from being the most bigoted Protectionist in the universe, became the champion of Free Trade.

Cobden advocated another principle, with equal fervour, but with by no means equal success. England, he contended, had no business whatever to mix herself up with European politics; her mission was to trade, not to fight. Therefore she should disband her forces and substitute non-interference for her foreign policy.

Now, how came this rapid and radical change in commercial policy about? And why was it not accompanied by an equally radical change in foreign policy? Why did not war estimates follow the Protective tariffs? Cobden was as much right upon one point as upon the other, *logically*. Why then was only half his scheme listened to? Why was he reverenced during commerce debates as the apostle of Free Trade, and laughed at when the army and navy estimates came on as the man with a hobby? Expediency: this one word answers all these questions. England could not feed her people, therefore she must encourage food imports. England wanted raw material for her multitudinous industries, therefore she must encourage imports of raw material. England could laugh at foreign competition in manufactures, thanks to her coal, and her iron, and her vast industrial capital, and the skill of her workmen, therefore she need not tax manufactured imports. But England must keep a firm hold on, and a clear road to, her foreign possessions: "the balance of power must be maintained," which means, that foreign and possibly hostile nations must be made to balance and neutralise each other's aggressive power; and her extensive shipping interests must be vigilantly guarded. Besides, Jem Mace's pithy advice, "If you want to avoid rows, learn how to box," or, as the Roman sage more elegantly phrased it, "*Si vis Pacem para Bellum,*" is sufficiently corroborated by national history, as well as by individual experience, to shelve the disarmament hobby. Fortunate England, that could thus combine her own best interests with the adoption of "broad, sound principles of moral right," as some one has sonorously expressed it! Prudent England, to temper even concessions to moral right with additions to the royal navy! *Soyous candides.* So long as England could feed her own population and supply her own factories with raw material, she was Protectionist to the core. Had she possessed sufficient area and sufficient resources to keep up these supplies, Free Trade would never have been dug out from the mine of theories known as "the wealth of nations," either by Richard Cobden, or by John Bright, or by anybody else.

Tempora mutantur et nos mutamur in illis. The United States, which secured their ultimate independence through a struggle, at first fought for Free Trade, have since then developed into the most determined upholders of Protection. Expediency again. The language of Cobden was as intelligible to Americans as to Englishmen, but (perhaps because they were not so hungry) they had ears for that portion only of his logic which England ignored— the economic folly of large armaments. Free Trade they would have nothing whatever to do with. Did they thereby consult their own best interests or not? A problem not to be answered by pointing to American Trade returns since (inasmuch as we have no means of knowing that America would not have thriven even faster under Free Trade) this merely begs the question. A problem, moreover, which, even did we possess this knowledge of what *would have happened*, could not be solved by a comparison of figures. It is one which mainly concerns the American people, and must, therefore, be regarded from an American platform. National interests are not *wholly* a matter of £ s. d.

When England adopted Free Trade, what was America's position? An area of nearly four million square miles, and comprising sufficient variety of soil, climate, and mineral wealth to furnish well-nigh every product of human industry; a country capable of some day supporting many hundreds of millions of persons, actually peopled by some twenty-five millions. A constant stream of immigration pouring in. A food supply covering all local demands and leaving a large margin for exportation. A rapidly-increasing production of raw material also available—*for exportation?* Why for exportation? Why not for home use? Because, by the very simplest Trade arithmetic, if America manufactured, she must do so at a loss. Why, then, manufacture at all? *Why not devote herself to producing and exporting raw material for England to manufacture?* Ah! now we have come at the root of the matter.

Trade means to exchange commodities for other

commodities or their equivalent value — if possible. Practically, trade has for its object to buy as cheap, and sell as dear as possible. When England buys America's raw material, say her cotton, she buys "cheap," *i.e.* she pays as little as she can help for it. If, now, America bought England's manufactures, say the same cotton worked up into calico, would she be buying cheap or dear? Look at the thing straight. America sells England £1,000 worth of cotton, and buys back the same cotton converted into calico for £4,000: which has the better of the deal? Of course theorists here step in with a summary and contemptuous reply. "Neither!" they cry. "The £3,000 difference merely represents the cost of transforming cotton into calico. The calico is as cheap at £4,000 as the cotton was at £1,000, because it cost only £1,000 to grow the cotton at a profit, whereas it cost £4,000 to manufacture it, also at a profit. In such an instance we merely have an example of the mutual benefits of trade." Very well; but, after all, America has *received* only £1,000, or its value, and has paid away £4,000, or its value. What has become of the £3,000? *Who has got it?* Has it not gone towards the support of English workmen, or the profits of the English manufacturer? Admitting that they all only barely get a living out of it, that the American capitalist grower gets even a higher rate of interest than the English capitalist manufacturer for his invested capital, and that the goods are excellent and cheap, does it not, after all, mean £4,000 *devoted to English manufacturing interests as against* £1,000 *devoted to American Raw Production?* "Oh!" again cries theory, "such a query simply presupposes utter ignorance of the most elementary economic facts." [Pardon, my dreamy friends, theories, *not* facts.] "If England can turn out an excellent article cheap, she is entitled to manufacturing pre-eminence. So long as she can produce goods at a *minimum* cost, she must and ought to be the chief source of the world's supply." Now, whether she *ought* is a point which Americans have declined even to discuss; whether she *must*, they have, so far as *their* section of the globe is concerned, pretty thoroughly disproved. And are they not justified, if they choose, in trying to build up manufacturing interests of their own with this balance? True, they cannot manufacture so cheaply as England *now*, perhaps they may not be able to do so for many years, perhaps (rather a probable "perhaps") they never will be able to do so. Is that a sufficient reason for not making the attempt? Not, at all events, in American eyes. We are, say our go-ahead kinsmen, a great nation, and we are destined to become the greatest nation upon earth; we are not a province tied on to the apron-strings of any other nation. We have an extent of territory that constitutes us practically a new world. We have no more business to be dependent upon the old world than we have to be dependent upon the moon; and we mean to be independent of creation. To do that, we must not only grow but manufacture what we require. At first, no doubt, we shall be manufacturing at a heavy figure, certainly at a heavier figure than some other nations. The profits, no doubt also, will not, at first, be extensive; but, great or small, we intend to keep them at home. If we prefer paying a high price for native-made goods to paying a low price for foreign goods, that's our own affair. A man may, without being a fool, pay his son five dollars for a box which he could buy, perhaps better made, for three dollars in a shop. He may say, " I want my boy to learn how to use his tools. I know he can't make the box for three dollars, and that others can. Still, I prefer paying the additional money, which remains in the family, and letting him get both the profit and the experience."

This unbounded faith of Americans in the future of America is a characteristic which even the most cold-blooded exponent of the " dismal science " can neither deride nor argue down. It is not sentiment— or at least if it is, it is very high-minded sentiment, vastly ahead of the sickly affectation of cosmopolitanism so distinctive of the John Bright school.

America is, from her geographical position, tolerably secure from becoming involved in foreign wars. Still complications *might* arise and cannot be totally ignored as impossible. Suppose they did, and suppose that America were dependent upon Europe for manufactured commodities. Suppose (*absit omen!*) England were against her. Result? Very complete blockade of all American ports, and stoppage of all foreign imports. To guard against this contingency, America might, indeed, if she chose, maintain a powerful fleet. She very sensibly prefers to set off the cost of this would-be necessary fleet against her losses from local manufactures, make herself, by means of these manufactures, independent of foreign supplies, and find subject-matter for Sunday discourse in the folly and wickedness of national armaments. If England tried to blockade the ports of manufacture against independent America, she would simply be cutting her own throat by cutting off her own factories from their chief source of raw material.

There is no getting away from the conclusion that the Americans are right from their point of view. America cannot be judged by any other standard than herself; she stands as yet alone among nations. With a population already exceeding the *European* population of any other nation, she is still but an infant to the America of the future. To compare her policy with that of tiny, overpeopled England, dependent for the very bread she eats upon her foreign Trade, is as irrational as it is fruitless. Protection is as expedient for America as Free Trade is necessary to England.

The further question, for what length of time should America adhere to this policy? does not come within our province to examine, and may be dismissed with the reflection that so soon as American manufactures can compete in Free Trade markets in any particular commodity, the continued necessity for protecting that commodity ceases to be very evident. Of that, however, the Americans are the best judges. What we now wish to direct attention to, is that the example of the United States is a very dangerous one for less considerable communities to follow. The frog who wanted to become like unto the ox came, as we read, to sudden and unexpected disintegration—a reminiscence which, without any intentional reflection upon the dignity of any existing British Dependency, brings us nearer home. We have now to state, as clearly as we can and as exhaustively as our limits will permit, the considerations upon which (if our conception be correct) the Colonies should decide between Protection and Free Trade. And these considerations should stand out with convincing clearness if only the following questions can be satisfactorily answered.

1. Is it possible for Australasia or Canada, as at present constituted, successfully to tread in the footsteps of the United States?

2. Would it be possible by altering their present Constitution?

3. Would such a course be conducive to their present or prospective advantage?

4. Can any alternative course be indicated offering greater immediate or future advantages?

1. *Is it possible for the Colonies, as at present constituted, successfully to tread in the footsteps of the United States?*

To this question (again protesting our utter innocence of intentionally wounding the national vanity of any British community) we reply, Irishwise, by asking another: Can a team of mules, all tugging in different directions, draw a load which it has required the combined efforts of a more numerous and more powerful team of horses to shift?

2. *Would it be possible by altering their present Constitution?*

If they changed their team? Certainly it would.

The seven Colonies of Australasia, for example, possess far greater initial advantages in 1891 than did the original thirteen Colonies of America when, upon the 7th June, 1776, Richard Henry Lee formulated his resolution (adopted by the Congress of these Colonies upon July 4th of the same year) that " The United Colonies are and ought to be free and independent States; and their political connection with Great Britain is and ought to be dissolved." Let us briefly compare the positions. Land? Australasia covers 3,169,000 square miles; the United States began with less than 600,000 square miles. Population? Nearly the same numerically; but, with modern facilities of transport and locomotion, and with modern labour-saving machinery, capable of achieving incomparably greater productive results. Capital? Beyond all comparison, in favour of Australasia. Upon what grounds can it therefore be doubted that if Australasia started upon the American lines, she would achieve a success, at least, equal to theirs? But—she must weigh well what those lines mean. They mean the proclamation to the whole world of an Independent Australasian nationality. They mean the Federal Union of all the Colonies of Australasia, which, by the way, it would be expedient, if not necessary, to subdivide into more numerous States. They mean a Supreme

Central Legislature by whose enactments the national policy must be shaped. They mean that this policy, once adopted by the delegates of a majority of States, must be binding upon all, else the Central Congress becomes a farce and the Union a dream. Protection is one such question of policy. Free Trade is another. The choice between the two, if the American model be copied, will be like Hobson's, and by that choice all must be bound. Upon this point the history of the American nation is clear and emphatic. The stability of the United States has received many rude shocks, and always upon the same question of national commercial policy—Protection or Free Trade. From the "Whisky War" in 1794 to the terrible civil struggle which began in February, 1861, the point at issue has always been the same—Protection or Free Trade. The Southern States, as the great producers of raw material, and as having few manufactures of their own, objected to the Protective duties imposed, by authority of Congress, upon foreign manufactured goods, simply, as they averred, in order that the Northern States might reap the profits of a monopoly in manufactures. This was the *causa teterrima belli.* The No-Slavery cry was a cloak[1]—not a sham altogether, for slavery *was*

[1] The genuine extent of the northern sympathy for "coloured brethren" has shown itself pretty plainly *since* the war. The

opposed to northern ideas in the abstract—to cover the really vital issue, Protection or Free Trade. "A house divided against itself shall surely fall." Had this division been effected, had the Confederate States been permitted to secede from the Union, or had they been able, by force of arms, to uphold their secession, their avowed intention was to adopt Free Trade. To prevent the division, to maintain the Union, to preserve Protection, the north unhesitatingly plunged into war—war upon a scale so gigantic, so profuse of blood and treasure, that the campaigns of Wellington seem but as skirmishes in comparison. Protection triumphed—but at what a cost! And it is upon these lines that the United States of Australasia would have to follow if America be their model. Like America, they must be prepared to rely upon their own resources, and to suffer the heavy temporary losses; at all events, inseparable, as we have seen, from Protective encouragement of native industries, in order that they may eventually become, like America, independent of foreign supplies. They must cease to regard Protection and Free Trade as

utter contempt of the Yankee for the "nigger," his marked avoidance of him, his distinct objection to eat with him, or drink with him, or even travel in the same carriage with him, are traits of race-prejudice which the most Conservative Britisher could not exceed.

rival systems, concerning which there may be a difference of opinion. They must consecrate Protection as the basis of the national policy, a basis to be upheld, if need arise, at the point of the bayonet. If Australasia is prepared to do and suffer all these things, then assuredly nothing but a convulsion of nature can prevent her from becoming *in time* the mighty southern rival of the mighty west.[1]

3. *Would such a course be conducive to their present or prospective advantage?*

To their present advantage, obviously *not*. Extravagant production *must* mean immediate loss. Bread cast upon the waters of Protection cannot return until after many days. To their prospective advantage then? That hinges altogether upon the meaning given to the word "advantage." If it be merely a matter of £ s. d., of profit and loss, then the probabilities *pro* or *con* can only be estimated by annotating the chief factors of *actual* national wealth, for of course the *potential* wealth (that is, the existing but undeveloped natural resources) of a country cannot be affected by national polity. Well, these chief factors of actual national wealth are briefly:

(I.) The extent, quality, and distribution of cur-

---

[1] *Mutatis mutandis*, the reasoning applied to Australasia applies with equal force to Canada.

rent production, including, of course, land, labour, and capital.

(II.) The excess of *profitable* production over local cousumption.

(III.) The facilities enjoyed for finding a market abroad for this excess of profitable production; that is, the means of carrying on a Foreign Trade.

(IV.) The accumulation of the results of past production, home or foreign.

(V.) Capital invested in unproductive property.

(VI.) National credit.

(VII.) The precious metals used as exchange-medium, *i.e.* the amount of "money" in circulation or available.

Now, it is not essential that all these factors should co-exist in order that a nation may be wealthy, a consideration of the very utmost importance which Economists seem to have overlooked. Or, perhaps, it would be more accurate to say, that a particular community may advantageously concentrate its efforts upon certain of these factors, regarding the others as of secondary importance. For instance, whilst the first is of paramount importance to Protectionist America, the second and third are absolutely essential to Free Trade England.

To a young, struggling community, again, national credit often means success or failure, national progress or national stagnation. To which of them should Australasia or Canada mainly pin her faith? They are all of them good things—very good things; but unfortunately it is, as we shall proceed to demonstrate, impossible to secure them *all* in equal degree. The first is peculiarly characteristic of, and consequent upon, Protection. The two next are equally peculiarly characteristic of, and consequent upon, Free Trade. The others depend upon the amount of success consequent upon the adoption of either policy.

(I.) *Extent, quality, and distribution of current production.*—Protection, being avowedly designed to make a community self-supporting and independent of foreign supplies, can obviously only hope to succeed in this design by the most strenuous local productive efforts. The primary, all-engrossing object is to meet all home demands without having recourse to foreign aid. And, if the theory of Protection be followed to its highest imaginable pitch of perfection, once this object is secured, there remains no incentive to devote any considerable attention to Foreign Trade. If one can suppose a community to be practically independent of all other communities for commodities, what could it accept in exchange for any surplus it might wish to export? Other commodities? *What* other commodities, if it already supplied all its own wants? Besides, consistent Protection *excludes* foreign commodities. Money? Money is mere dross once its exchange-value disappears. Such luxuries, etc., as could not, even conceivably, be produced by any one community? Yes, *they* might be accepted; *and they would represent the total foreign-trade interest of the community.* Ideal Protection would transmute " Happy the nation which has no history," into " Happy the nation which has no [necessity for] Foreign Trade." Alas for ideal Protection! Bursting its patriotic heart, straining its every fibre to secure Dead Sea fruit; foregoing an immediate tangible certainty to follow a distant theoretical possibility; dropping, like Æsop's dog, the meat of Trade to grasp at the shadow of Independence! It is not, of course, inferred that because a community adopts Protection, it must necessarily strain after any such ideal, and neglect its foreign trade. But to judge a policy by the very utmost ultimate advantages it has to offer is a perfectly legitimate course, as indicating the *tendency*, at all events, of that policy. And judged by this standard, Protection must *tend* to concentrate its energies upon multitudinous branches of local production, and, in comparison, to underrate its Foreign Trade.

On the other hand, a Free Trade community will only pay such particular attention to its current production as its individual, natural and other advantages may seem to suggest. It is under no sort of obligation to produce everything which it consumes. It will, indeed, not attempt to produce anything which it cannot turn out at a minimum cost. It views the whole earth as productively its own. It cares nothing where commodities come from. It knows but one rule for production: "Make the best use of natural advantages." If it can most profitably produce raw material, it will produce raw material; if it can most profitably manufacture, it will manufacture. If it can, to a certain extent, profitably do both, it will, to that extent, do both.

(II.) *Excess of profitable production over local consumption.*—The word "profitable" at once puts Protection out of court so far as this factor is concerned. Protection produces everything at a loss, judged by the value of the things produced in the world's markets, as compared with the cost of their production. Were it otherwise, there would be no necessity to exclude foreign competition. Therefore, the greater the excess of local production over local requirements, the greater the loss; which proves once more, and by a different road, a previously connoted fact, *viz.*, that overproduction is the Nemesis of Protection.

To Free Trade this excess means the stock available for purposes of exchange, and is, therefore, the backbone of the system. What that stock may consist of, whether of raw material, or of manufactured goods, or of both, will, of course, once more depend upon the special producing advantages enjoyed by each Free Trade community. But raw, or manufactured, or both, the surplus represents that portion of the national wealth devoted to the purpose of securing, at the cheapest cost, those commodities which the community cannot itself produce at a minimum expense. And hence, the greater the excess of profitable local production over local requirements, the greater the quantity of foreign produce which will be secured.

(III.) *Facilities enjoyed for finding a market abroad for this excess of profitable production; that is, the means of carrying on a Foreign Trade.*—It may be objected that, if our position is sound, and if Protective production be *really*, as well as apparently, a losing game (even though possibly, for national reasons, justifiable upon the score of expediency), Protective nations would soon abandon Foreign Trade altogether, and that most certainly they would never be such fools as to encourage locally-owned foreign-going shipping to their own disadvantage. This objection would have some force if it could also be shown that Protective communities understand the *real drift* of their policy. But they do not, because the fallacies of Protection do not lie upon the surface, because it is the most plausible fraud that ever blinded men's better judgment. The unthinking, long-suffering "protected" many are the victims of the keen-sighted *protected* few. The *protected* manufacturer often makes "his pile" out of goods for which the "protected" consumer pays twice their value. It matters nothing to the manufacturer that the community *as a whole* is losing, so long as he can feather his own nest. He may even, under the mantle of Protection, produce to such advantage in *special lines*, as to be able to compete in Free Trade markets, *and still enjoy Protection at home!* There is absolutely no limit to the public blindness if only sufficient dust be thrown in its eyes, and patriotism is a caster which holds a lot of dust. But the really fatal flaw in the above objection is, that it seeks to disprove by a *reductio ad absurdum*, what really takes place. The conclusions to which common-sense analysis of cause and effect points are abundantly confirmed by statistics. Four-fifths of the international trade of the world is carried in Free Trade bottoms. If we take particular instances, the matter assumes a still clearer aspect. Eighty-three per cent. of the international commerce of the United States is carried on in Free Trade ships. Or, to take a

Colonial example, whereas Victoria, before she adopted Protection, owned three times as much shipping as New South Wales, New South Wales now owns more than twice as much shipping as Victoria. Or, if we glance at the register of Free Trade England, we find figures which almost challenge belief. The Foreign Trade alone of England, exclusive altogether of her vast local coasting-trade, employs British vessels with an aggregate burden of 10,241,856 tons! Now, hereby hangs a tale. The profits of the carrying Trade are enormous, the mere ship-building industry is enormous, the number of men employed both to make and to work these ships is enormous, everything in any way connected with shipping is upon an enormous scale. Of these advantages Free Trade has practically a monopoly, a monopoly not of her own seeking or due to any superior enterprise of Free Trade communities, but because hers is essentially a Trade policy. The Americans are proverbially cute and "go ahead." Yet, their foreign-going shipping is but a fraction of England's, and much even of that has to "cadge" for freights in Free Trade ports. So also their Foreign Trade is but a fraction of England's.[1] And all who imitate their policy must be prepared like them to see their Foreign Trade become a merely subsidiary item of their national wealth.

[1] See appendix note on Foreign Trade.

(IV.) *The accumulation of the results of past production, home and foreign.*—Both sorts, of course, represent wealth, but whereas under Protection the increment is synonymous with over-production and stagnation for want of a natural outlet—a sort of productive white elephant,—under Free Trade it simply means temporary withdrawal of capital from a particular industry, or industries, until the accumulation shall have been dispersed through Trade. The difference between an overflowing cistern with a choked plug-hole and a full cistern with a clear 'scape-pipe is sufficiently obvious, especially if *the former* is supplied from a *tap that cannot be turned off.*

(V.) *Capital invested in unproductive property.*—Under this category will of course come plate, jewellery, pictures, furniture, yachts, race-horses, and the thousand and one other luxuries of civilised life. All this capital is of course practically idle from a productive point of view; but it exists, it is always available at a national pinch, and cannot therefore be overlooked. What chiefly concerns us at present is the reflection that, *cæteris paribus*, the more cheaply a community obtains its necessaries, the more it will have to expend upon luxuries (so obnoxious to the dismal school) that help to make life "worth living." Free Trade communities have evidently a decided advantage here. What say figures? They are simply powerless to give us an adequate idea of the unused wealth of Free Trade England. The accumulation of plate alone is upon a scale almost fabulous. The royal collection represents three and a half millions sterling. It has been estimated, upon such information as could be obtained, that the total value of the gold and silver sunk in the form of "plate" in the United Kingdom exceeds *one hundred million pounds sterling!* Of the value of the jewellery from the regalia to the workman's watch, not even an approximation has yet been made. So of the other items. They *must* represent many hundreds of millions. America is by comparison hopelessly in the rear. She can, indeed, point to a few millionaires (Protection is a regular nursery for the few) who, in her own expressive idiom, "make things hum" in the way of costly magnificence. But by the time her people have paid "through the nose" for their Protected commodities, they cannot afford to let much of their capital lie idle.

(VI.) *National Credit.*—This is a factor which may be either of the very gravest importance or of comparative insignificance, according to the actual financial requirements of particular communities, depending, in fact, upon the necessity, or absence of necessity, of borrowing foreign capital. Neither Protected America nor Free Trade England, for example requires foreign assistance. If, owing to any unforeseen emergency, money is wanted for national purposes, it can at once be obtained in New York or in London. But certain other communities are not so independent. They are always wanting money, and, as the London Stock Exchange knows pretty well, they are not at all backward in asking for it. Now, as all hard-up communities apply, with unfailing regularity, to the same source, a certain amount of competition is engendered. John Bull lends very freely; he is fond of lending when he sees (or thinks he sees) decent security and good interest. In times gone-by he has sometimes allowed himself to look too lovingly at the interest and not critically enough at the security. Most of the States of South America have bled him horribly. He would be glad to have all the money he has lent to Argentina, and Turkey, and Egypt safe back in his coffers. He is getting more careful. He is making up his mind very fast to leave Mexico severely alone, and invest his savings in his own colonies. Australasia is just now a prime favourite. The alacrity with which loan after loan is subscribed for amazes even agents-general. One hundred and sixty-three millions have already found their way out there in the shape of loans, and *apparently* as much more could be had for the asking. But appearances are proverbially deceptive, and national credit is a very ticklish affair. Once let a country show symptoms of radical unsoundness, and that country's credit sinks like a stone. John Bull is a thorough believer in Free Trade. By its means he has become what he is—a head and shoulders financially taller than any one else. He utterly loathes Protection, because he holds it to be rotten to the core, and because it hampers his Trade. He cannot, indeed, well deny that America has got on very well under Protection; but, from his point of view, she has done so *in spite of* Protection; and he chuckles when he compares his trade and his shipping with hers. Moreover, America has no political connection with him, and does not often come to him for loans, and so her policy he has no business to criticise. But with his own colonies the case is very different. He does not assume a right to dictate what policy they shall pursue; but he has no sympathy with those who repudiate *his* policy. So long, indeed, as a Protective colony can manage to pay interest on previous loans, he does not refuse further advances; he lends, marvelling the while at the borrower's wrongheadedness. But once let such a colony get into serious monetary troubles, and that colony is financially damned. J. B., as a Free Trader, will attribute the disasters to Protection, and button up his pockets. To a Free Trade colony he cannot but be more indulgent. Nothing short of absolute national bankruptcy would shake his confidence in Free Trade New South Wales. He saw her a year ago with a large deficit and apparently very hard-pushed, and he subscribed for her five and a half million loan *many times over*, at lowest current rates. Why? Simply because she is his pet; her policy is his policy, and that policy, in his eyes, cannot mislead. Could Victoria, after showing a budget deficiency of over a million, expect similar favour? The whole affair is so very plain: does not every creditor like to feel secure that his debtor's business is worked upon a sound basis? And what is true of national credit, as affecting national borrowing-power, is true, in a still more marked degree, of private enterprise. English capital must, in the long run, be principally drawn to those countries which model their policy upon English lines. And when we come to reflect that the Colonies are, to a very large measure, dependent upon borrowed capital, the importance of a policy which shall attract that capital freely presents itself in very strong colours indeed.

(VII.) *The precious metals used as exchange-medium.*—A very marked and distinct factor of national wealth, which Protection professes to esteem very lightly, preferring to make use of a fictitious currency. The idea is (and a thoroughly Protectionist idea it is) to obviate the necessity of an expensive and rapidly wearing-out coinage by substituting Government guaranteed paper money. It is not a new idea; it has been put forward over and over again, especially by the "three-acres-and-a-cow-per-man" class of social reformers. It has, like most demagogue solutions of economic problems, the merit of extreme simplicity. When "hard times" come, cannot Government issue plenty of paper money and make every one's heart glad? The ludicrous absurdity of thus endowing a Government with the supernatural power of imparting *intrinsic* value to scraps of paper, which are *not* promises to pay, *on demand*, in coin value, need not here be dwelt upon. Those who have never given the question of Exchange any particular attention will find an appendix note[1] to guide them in fixing their ideas. Our immediate business is to point out that Free Trade distinctly recognises the necessity of having an *intrinsically* valuable coinage and a standard as far removed as possible from serious fluctuations in value. The English coinage is such a coinage, and the English "sovereign" is such a standard—a standard typical of the wealth-supremacy of Free Trade England.

The preceding paragraphs have treated the question of "advantage" from a purely £ s. d. point of view.

[1] See appendix note on Exchange.

But it may, on the other hand, be regarded from the American standpoint—as a matter of national feeling, of patriotism. It then, of course, passes beyond the province of argument altogether, and into the realms of sentiment. Independent nationality, even with small beginnings, may to some seem the noblest expression of Australasian or Canadian ambition. But how does it appear to the majority of Australasians and Canadians? Is the game of future greatness worth the candle of present loss? The voice of the Australasian and Canadian peoples can alone answer the question. If that voice answers in the affirmative, if nothing short of absolute independence will satisfy Colonial aspirations, then Protection, with all its radical defects, its inherent unsoundness, steps into the arena clothed in the invulnerable armour of expediency, against which not even Free Trade can prevail; history simply repeats itself; the United States of Australasia and of Canada have the same future before them as had the United States of America one hundred and fourteen years ago.

4. *Can any alternative course be indicated offering greater immediate or future advantages?*

Yes, both immediate and future; and that course is—Federal Union with England. Let but the Colonies decide, and give open expression to the decision, that it is NOT a nobler ambition to erase the glorious old name "British" from the national records and become an ethnological *Olla Podrida* than to retain the race ties of blood and kinship and become States of the Britannic Confederation—let them but do this, and the great problem will be solved. Public opinion both in England and in the Colonies has decided, in very pronounced tones, that the present disjointed, incoherent condition of the Empire must forthwith be remodelled. The wisest heads in England have, for some time past, been trying to discover how this reform may best be effected, but no plan acceptable to all concerned has as yet been formulated. Colonial agents-general (who, by the way, ought to have "*Ne sutor ultra Crepidam*" tacked on to their K.C.M.G. brevets, or they will soon blossom forth as ministers-plenipotentiary) have been simply begging the real question by feeble suggestions about Imperial-manned, Colonial-paid squadrons and other trivialities. The subject of Federation has been, and is, receiving the most careful attention from English statesmen, from the English press, and from the English public. The only conclusion so far arrived at has been that Federation proposals must come from the Colonies to England and not from England to the Colonies!

Now, there must be some reason for this seeming

inability of English brain-power to solve a problem which, though certainly difficult, is also certainly very far from being insuperable. Where is the stumbling-block? Inability to formulate a merely technical scheme? Surely not; any clerk in the Colonial office could do that. The "Irish difficulty?" Then why not embody it in the solution? The most probable explanation would seem to be in the fact that England and the Colonies are at variance upon the question of Commercial Policy. England hitherto has been definitely, wholly pledged to Free Trade; her commercial supremacy has depended upon it. Most of the Colonies are trying to "play upon their own hands" *(more Americano)*, and are steeped in Protection. Now, if Federation of the Empire is to be effected at all, it must be thorough, and it must be based upon three things:

(I.) Local self-government of all Federal States.

(II.) Representation of these States in a central Imperial Parliament.

(III.) Unity of commercial polity.

The first practically exists already. The second merely needs a royal warrant to spring into existence. The third has been, and still is, the real stumbling-block.

And here for the moment we pause. We have glanced at the rival systems from almost every possible aspect, and we have found that Free Trade everywhere emerges triumphant. But we have also seen that, although always the soundest, it is not always the most expedient policy. We have hereafter, therefore, to see whether or not it would be the expedient policy for a Britannic Confederation. And this will form the subject of discussion throughout the Empire for perhaps many years to come.

APPENDIX NOTES.

"FAIR TRADE."

THE MILLER AND THE BAKERS: A FABLE.

There once lived a miller, named Protection, looked upon by his own family as a model father, but spoken of by strangers as a selfish, grasping sort of fellow, who would, any-day, rather waste time and spoil good leather trying to make himself a pair of boots, than buy them in a shop. At some distance from the mill resided two bakers, Free Trade and Fair Trade, who had been in the habit for years of getting most of their flour from Protection, although the covetous miller tried hard to do all his own baking at home, and seldom bought so much as a biscuit from either of his customers. One day both bakers called on him to remonstrate with him upon his selfishness. He heard all they had to say, did not deny that his home-made bread was neither so good nor so cheaply made as their bread, but absolutely refused to alter his tactics. "If you like," he said, "to buy my surplus flour, you can; if not, you can leave it alone. I'm not dependent upon the mill for a living; and I tell you straight that I'd rather pay dear for home-made bread than cheap for your bread. I have a fancy for home-made bread.... I want my family to learn how to make bread...... there may be a smash-up amongst you bakers some day, and I may have to rely on my own ovens altogether. Suppose any reasons you like, but take my answer—No." Whereupon Fair Trade got very red in the face and answered hotly, "Then if you won't buy my bread, I'll not buy your flour. There are plenty of other millers in the world. They can't perhaps sell quite so cheaply as you, but they're not such selfish brutes. And I've made up my mind for the future to buy only from those who buy from me!" And Fair Trade went away highly exasperated. "Well," said Protection to Free Trade, somewhat anxiously, though he tried to look unconcerned, "what are *you* going to do? Boycott my flour too?" "Not I!" replied Free Trade. "As we say in my trade, 'half a loaf is better than no bread.' You do your best to take half my trade loaf from me by refusing me your custom; but you must, for your own sake, leave me the other half—your supply of flour. Do you suppose I'm such a fool as to refuse *half* a good thing because I can't get the *whole?* I repeat, miller, that your jack-of-all-trades notions are simply absurd. As a man of sense, not to say as a *baker*, it seems to me rank insanity to turn out home-made rubbish for 8d. which you could buy, best quality, for 5d. But that's your loss chiefly. As for me, I will buy my flour from you so long as you can undersell other millers. If at any time you require a cake, or biscuits, or even a *decently-made loaf*, don't forget that I'm the best and cheapest baker in the world. Good-day." "Yah!" roared the miller, much incensed at this parting shot. "You'll buy from me because you can't supply your own flour; no thanks to *you!*" "None whatever," returned Free Trade, cheerily, as he disappeared down the street.

"Don't forget the address!" And thus it came to pass that baker Fair Trade did a small mutual back-scratching business and gratified his anger against the miller, while Free Trade did a roaring commerce with the whole world.

The moral of this little fable is very obvious. In whatever light we may choose to regard Fair Trade as a question of sentiment, as a pure matter of business it has not a leg to stand upon, except (like its first-cousin, Protection) *expediency*. Moreover, it could only be justified, even from motives of expediency, *as a powerful lever to uproot Protection;* and it would have to be adopted by a large number of widely-scattered, widely-producing communities, else supplies of raw material would be utterly inadequate. It might, for example, be deemed *expedient* for all States and Dependencies of the Britannic Confederation to adopt Fair Trade tactics in their dealings with foreign nations. Such a course, although it would entail present loss upon British States proportionate to the inability of even our well-distributed Empire to supply *all* commodities at a minimum cost, would, on the other hand, *compel Protectionist nations either to open their ports or abandon foreign trade altogether*. It would then become merely a question of time how long Protection could be bolstered up. Of the ultimate result there can be no conceivable doubt. Whether the final triumph of Free Trade would be cheaply purchased at a temporary productive loss it would be for the Confederate States to determine. Fair Trade, upon a small scale, is too ludicrous for serious comment.

HENRY GEORGE ON FREE TRADE.

THE name of Henry George carries weight with the masses, and not undeservedly, for he is a conscientious and very persistent advocate of what he believes to be their best interests. Like Cobden, a self-made, self-taught man, he possesses, also like Cobden, great natural clearness of perception and fluency of expression. Unfortunately, once more like Cobden, he has a hobby; and, just as the "Apostle of Free Trade" could not return thanks after an agricultural dinner without introducing a stray slap or two at his pet aversion—national armaments, so, too, Mr. George never misses an opportunity of dragging *his* bugbear—uneven division and tenure of land—into every subject which he approaches. "National armaments," thundered Cobden, "are a wicked waste of national wealth, an exhausting drain upon the resources of the nation : therefore national armaments ought to be abolished." "The existing systems of land tenure," argues Mr. George, "are the causes of all social troubles; they are based upon principles utterly inconsistent with natural right : therefore they ought to be swept away." Mr. George is perfectly right, as was also Mr. Cobden,—theoretically. His position is quite unassailable judged by the standard of right and wrong. But he is not satisfied with theoretical accuracy; he hammers away unceasingly at a right which no one denies : whereby he becomes insufferably wearisome, and ends by running his head against the stone wall called expediency. No sane man nowadays disputes that nine-tenths of all civilised institutions are radically at variance with natural right. Tenure of land is merely one instance out of thousands. Of what use can it be to write volume after volume in proof of a self-evident truth? Mr. Henry George has, so far, persistently committed the grave error of leaving off where he ought to begin; this eternal "slaying the corpse" of natural right is quite unworthy a prophet of his pretensions. If he would direct his attacks against his live enemy, expediency, he would at least save much valuable time. His latest work upon Free Trade is a repetition of the old song, in a different key. His naturally acute perceptions enable him vividly to realise the intrinsic excellence of Free Trade, although, as he confesses, he commenced his investigations with strong Protective prejudices. Indeed, he goes so far as to deny to Protection the one claim which, from our point of view, it may be said to possess in the case of the United States—expediency.

"In the early days of the American Republic, when the friends of Protection were trying to ingraft it upon the Federal revenue system, Protection was asked, not for the maintenance of American industry, but for the establishment of 'infant industries,' which, it was asserted, would, if encouraged for a few years, be able to take care of themselves. The infant boys and girls of that time have grown to maturity, become old men and women, and with rare exceptions have passed away. The nation then fringing the

Atlantic seaboard has extended across the continent, and instead of four million now numbers nearly sixty million people. But the 'infant industries,' for which a little temporary Protection was then timidly asked, are still infants in their desire for encouragement. Though they have grown mightily, they claim the benefits of the 'Baby Act' all the more lustily, declaring that if they cannot have far higher Protection than at the beginning they dreamed of asking, they must perish outright. . . . When we are told that two generations should tax themselves to establish an industry for a third, well may we ask, 'What has posterity ever done for us?'"

Mr. George being himself an American, his opinion upon this point is of interest; but how far is his opinion a gauge of American sentiment generally? Judging from the immense popularity of the writer, we make no doubt that Mr. George's work will have proved to be a powerful contribution to the cause of Free Trade, though we are convinced that nothing short of Imperial Federal reciprocity will ever convert the United States. But we learn without surprise that, ably as the subject has been handled, it is used mainly as a peg whereon to hang reiterated denunciations of land tenure. Beggars on horseback have not a monopoly of reckless riding. Mount an enthusiast on his hobby, and he will ride it at anything. There is, however, comfort in the reflection that those who may be convinced by Mr. George's arguments of the inherent superiority of Free Trade over Protection are not compelled to follow him in his agrarian deviations.

FOREIGN TRADE.

That Protection is in its very nature destructive to Foreign Trade has, it is hoped, been made sufficiently clear. The subjoined returns are appended rather to illustrate than to confirm the inevitable results of a Protective policy. The statistics are for 1889.

States.	Population.	Total Trade.	Average per head.
United Kingdom*	38,910,000	£742,343,336	£19·1
United States	62,480,540	326,920,745	5·2
New South Wales*	1,122,000	46,157,991	41
Canada	5,200,000	42,002,877	8
Victoria	1,104,288	40,825,937	36
France	38,218,903	311,343,880	8·1
Germany	47,650,806	351,086,350	7·3
Austria-Hungary	41,827,700	104,870,000	2·5
Straits Settlements*	568,000	57,883,668	101·7
Italy	30,120,000	88,345,673	2·9
Channel Islands*	90,310	4,588,595	55

* Free Trade ; all the others Protectionist.

Figures certainly strip Protection rather bare. One hears a vast deal about Yankee smartness, push, enterprise, and so forth, but what about the Yankee Trade average? Certainly no one who has any knowledge of Americans will question the justice of their claim to the brilliant business qualities generally ascribed to them. One meets them everywhere. Their agents scour the world. Their fertility of resource, their indefatigable efforts to push their trade abroad, have become proverbial. And the result? £5 4s. per head. How pregnant of meaning are those two figures. What a tale they tell of the powerlessness of even the most strenuous efforts to withstand the destructive torrent of Protection! In the case of the apparently enormous Trade average of the Straits Settlements, it is only fair to point out that the figures must not be regarded from the same point of view as those of the other countries. Singapore, for instance, is really a large depôt for a considerable portion of the Eastern trade, and its profits are chiefly those of agents or middlemen, not those of producers. Still the fact remains that £57,883,673 worth of Trade passed in 1884 through the hands of the Straits people, because they have the good sense to keep their ports open—so very wide open, indeed, that *they levy duty upon nothing*. The splendid display made by the Straits in the Indian and Colonial Exhibition has frequently been mentioned by the London correspondents of leading Colonial journals in terms of wonder. Has it occurred to these gentlemen that the Colony in question shows larger Trade returns than any other British possession, except India? And this means a great deal, even making all due allowance for the special character of the Trade.

The returns of the other alien nations require little comment. It may be remarked that the countries enumerated have (excepting Austria-Hungary) plenty of sea-board: in land places, being under natural Trade disadvantages, have been purposely omitted. The large returns of Victoria and New South Wales point to the *immense importance of their foreign trade to both Colonies*, in the first place; and, further, suggest a very leading question. How comes it, in the face of the asserted tendency of Protection to destroy Trade, that Victoria's average not alone vastly exceeds that of the United States, but comes such a very respectable second to that of New South Wales? The answer is as simple as our limits compel it to be short. Victoria can no more become like the United States commercially than could our bull frog physically rival the ox; *she cannot live without Trade.* She may, indeed, like the United States, place herself at great Trade disadvantage, but she cannot, like the United States, be practically independent of other nations and afford to regard her Trade as a merely secondary consideration. A wealthy man with a craze may, if he likes, feed his cows upon green peas and cucumbers, and churn very dear butter. But what of the dairyman who imitates the example? *He* must sell butter—or close his dairy. But where are his *profits*, after his expensively-produced article has been sold in the open market? Are his home-slopped clothes and his home-cobbled boots a satisfactory set-off? One can understand an American chuckling over even his little £5 4s. average, because, small as it is, more than half of it is export—an important consideration, *under Protection.* But what about Victoria? She is avowedly only buying what she *can't* make, and she is selling less than she buys. Her "protected" children are therefore paying the maximum price for home-made goods, paying *ditto* for imported goods, getting only Free Trade prices for their exports, and paying heavy taxes besides! Surely the cause for wonderment is, *not* that she shows respectable total Trade returns—she *must* do that *at any cost;* but that she should be content to sacrifice her Trade profits at the shrine of her fetish. Better surely, if she *will* have Protection, follow America and be content with the American average, than drift to ruin upon a losing trade. It's easily done. Let her *cram on more Protection.* The result will speedily be to make it plain to all that she cannot stand alone, like her great model. And once it *is* made plain that no one Colony can dispense with Trade, it may then dawn upon the brains of even Protective enthusiasts that artificially bolstered-up, extravagant production is, and eternally must be, synonymous with commercial loss.

MANUFACTURES.

THE strongest supporters of Protection are naturally those who, through its means, enjoy the lion's share of productive monopoly; that is, the manufacturers and their *employés*. One may therefore be led to inquire what proportion these favoured individuals bear to the total population; and, fortunately, we have some statistics to enlighten us.

AMERICAN PROTECTED MANUFACTURES IN 1876-1886.

	1876	1886
Number of establishments	252,148	253,852
Capital	£338,913,403	£558,054,521
Hands employed	2,053,996	2,732,595
Value of materials	£398,148,358	£679,364,710
Value of products [1]	£677,172,070	£1,073,915,838

Now more than one-half of the establishments and of the capital, and nearly two-thirds of the workmen are in the States of New York, Pennsylvania, Ohio, Mass, Illinois, Indiana, and Michigan. This leaves the balance to be distributed among the *thirty-one other States and eight territories of the Union.* It was the monstrous monopoly

---

[1] *Local* value, of course, not *Trade* value. In Free Trade markets the average value would be 33 per cent. *at least*, less, *i.e.*, the *wasted cost of Protected production.*

that, as already noted, led to the secession of the Southern States. But apart from this, if we even *supposed* the manufactures to be fairly distributed, we find a still more glaring injustice in front of us. In 1876 the population of the United States amounted to 48,558,371, and every man, woman, and child of this number was paying exorbitant prices for commodities in order that two millions of persons might be permitted to charge their own rates. Ten years later the population had swollen to 56,155,783 souls, the "Protected" class to 2,732,595. The present population is estimated at 63,000,000; the operatives have not, even on paper, yet reached 3,000,000, while, of their real number, 370,000 are *actually out of employment.* The objection that to the number of operatives must also be added the women and children dependent on them is pointless, because even this addition would only result in a small fraction of the total population, and *all* are paying Protection rates, including the operatives themselves. The whole affair is utterly past argument. If the American *people*, the sixty odd millions of consumers, could, by some miracle, be made to understand the figures we have quoted, Protection would be thrown where the Protected tea was thrown in 1773—into Boston harbour.

An organ of the party which relies upon farmers' votes to sustain its policy of Protection (says the *Boston Herald*) admits that, "at the present price of wheat in Chicago, an ordinary western farmer cannot make a dollar a day raising it." The ordinary farmer cannot escape, however, paying a tariff tax averaging 46 per cent. upon his imported necessities. He pays 55 per cent. upon plain white earthenware, 65 per cent. upon window glass, 40 per cent. upon bags of bagging, 45 per cent. upon machinery and all manufactures of iron and steel, 35 per cent. upon matches, from 37 to 81 per cent. upon salt, 54 per cent. upon sugar, 2 dollars per 1,000 feet for boards and lumber, and an average of 66 per cent. upon the manufactures of wool used in his family. Truly "the farmer pays for all," and precious little does he get in return from "the highest tariff in the world."

Victoria, in her little bull-frog fashion, is trying hard to follow suit. This is how her manufactures stood in 1884:

Establishments, great and small,	2,856
Number of hands employed,	49,373
Capital (lands, buildings, machinery, and plant),	£10,199,918

Of the value of the manufactured products we can find no reliable returns. A Victorian estimate places it at £15,000,000, and as this approximates to the American ratio, it is perhaps nearly correct; though, of course, £15,000,000 worth of Victorian protected goods would "go at an alarming sacrifice" in Free Trade markets, and have therefore a very *fictitious value*. But let that pass. The population of the Colony in December 1884 was 961,276. We have therefore once more the overwhelming majority sacrificed to the theoretical (and utterly mistaken) advantage of the minority. Nay, in the case of Victoria the tyranny is intensified by the fact that all but a small fractional portion of the manufacturing interest is centred in one town—Melbourne. And yet the unthinking, hoodwinked hundreds of thousands of Victorian consumers allow themselves to be persuaded that they are in the very vanguard of industrial progress! A trade which, crippled as it is, and forced, as it is, *into the most unprofitable channels*, by Protection, still totals £40,825,937 *per annum*, a trade which, under Free Trade, would *double*[1] *itself in a few years* and *upon profitable lines*, strangled in order to bolster up ruinous "industries" which represent, even nominally, but ten millions of pounds, and are not, intrinsically, worth half the money!

[1] We use the word "double" advisedly. If Victoria adopted a Free Trade policy, the other Protective Colonies would follow suit, and the *general Trade* would increase, not by slow degrees, but by leaps and bounds. And a Free Trade Australia would assuredly go far to convert Protectionist Canada.

EXCHANGE AND CURRENCY.

EXCHANGE is the term applied in commerce to those transactions, the technical details of which we need not enter into, by which the debts of individuals, residing at a distance from one another, are settled, without the necessity of remitting specie. Evidently the trade between any two communities, representing the aggregate of individual liabilities, will not, if estimated for a fixed period, exactly balance; there will be a surplus owing from one to the other. This used, years ago, to be expressed by saying that the balance of trade was in favour of the one and against the other, that country being regarded as best off which exported more than it imported. It was further held to be an incontrovertible axiom that if the country which had the "balance" against it could not show imported specie to make up the deficiency, that country was in a bad way. This primitive way of regarding trade, especially the mysterious excellence attached to specie, survives now in the imaginations only of a few "Faddists." The law is now thoroughly well established by experience that EXCHANGE TENDS TO EQUILIBRIUM; indeed, when the exchange is really most favourable to a country, the tendency is to *increase that country's importation in order to restore equilibrium.* This, to the average reader, will not be very obvious, a fact the less to be wondered at inasmuch as exchange is, perhaps, the most complicated of all economic subjects. Of this complication Protectionists are not slow to take advantage. They profess to see one point standing out very clearly, namely, that a properly Protected country will buy very little and sell a great deal by closing its ports to imports and exporting its surplus. The rest of the subject is, they say, messed up in the fogs of Free Trade. Ingenious certainly, and superficially plausible, like most Protectionist theories, but fragile as a soap bubble beneath the touch of criticism.

1. *To illustrate the law itself.*—The gold produced in Victoria, say during the year 1852, required a certain amount of labour and capital for its production. An equal amount of labour and capital employed, during the same year, upon the production of, say, cotton, in a cotton-growing country, would not show a return equal in value to the Victorian gold. Therefore, temporarily, the equilibrium of exchange would be upset in favour of Victoria, which, we may even suppose, could produce gold with an exchange-value of £4 per oz., at a labour-capital outlay of perhaps only £1 5s. per oz. In the long run, however, according to the law, equilibrium will be restored; that is, it will be found that, upon an average, all the gold raised since gold-mining became an industry in Victoria, has cost £4 per oz. And even if it can be shown that the gold has cost, upon an average, only £3 10s. to produce, this fact would by no means contradict the law: it would merely prove that the exchange has been (as regards gold) upon a diminishing

scale in favour of Victoria ever since; or, in other words, that equilibrium has not yet been restored, but *is tending* rapidly towards it. If, on the other hand, gold (or any other product, from Geelong tweed to scented soap) *costs more than its exchange-value to produce*, then the equilibrium is upset *against* Victoria. It will, of course, *tend* to right itself if left free and unhampered by artificial restrictions, as naturally as a man dropping from a scaffolding will, by the law of gravitation, fall to the ground. If, however, its efforts towards equilibrium are choked by the continued pressure of the exciting cause of disturbance—Protection— it will, like a man whose descent is arrested by the tightening of a rope round his throat, *hang by the neck till it is dead.*

2. *Statistical returns are no guide whatever to the actual exchange position of a country.*—Why not? Because, in the first place, the expenses of transport are added to the estimated value of *exports* but not to the value of *imports*. Hence, many nations, with little or no carrying trade of their own, show a nominal excess of export over import-value, which, were the cost of freight deducted, would be reversed. Eighty-three per cent., for instance, of American exports are carried in foreign bottoms (nearly all English), and the real profit to America of these exports is their value after freight has been paid—to English shipowners. So, too, of other nations with whom England has commercial relations. England does by far the greatest portion of the world's carrying trade, and secures carriage profits which neither figure in her Trade returns nor in theirs, but which amount

(both ways) to nearly *one-third of the gross produce-value.* Nominal export-values are further misleading, owing to the fact that they are gauged locally (an absurd exaggeration in the case of Protected countries) and not by their selling or exchanging value, which is not ascertained till some time afterwards.

3. *The whole Export-Import Trade of a country must periodically be balanced.*—An insolvent nation may, for a time, import upon credit, just as an insolvent individual may live upon credit, but in the long run *both* must square up accounts or—face bankruptcy. Hence the well-observed fact that the exporting power of any nation, during a considerable consecutive number of years, is an accurate index to its importing power.

The absurdity of attempting to estimate Trade profits by subtracting imports from exports is pointed perhaps even more forcibly by the case of England than by discounting local exaggerations. The mother of nations *seems* to be placed above the necessity of even periodically balancing —since her imports *always* exceed her exports—on paper. A stock argument, this of Protectionists, according to whom England must be simply rushing headlong to national bankruptcy. They do not deem it necessary (or advisable) to point out that of English imports nearly £120,000,000 worth consists of food which could not be produced in England; that more than the nominal "balance against her" is simply transferred to her shipowners; that her enormous receipts in bullion do not figure in the returns; and that a comparatively small quantity of her exported manufactures represent, owing to increased value, a large quantity of imported raw material in value, thus leaving yearly an enormous margin for home consumption, besides a considerable yearly increment to the national wealth.

Collating now these various facts upon exchange, we are brought back to the first law that it tends to equilibrium; that it must in the long run attain equilibrium, unless artificially prevented; and that the national profit or loss during the intervals between tending and attainment, can only be estimated by the nation's total trade, tempered by its facilities for cheap production, cheap exchange, and cheap transport.

The subject of *Currency* is, so far as British Colonies are concerned, strictly speaking, beyond our present inquiry. It will be sufficient to indicate the strong Protective tendency to discard metallic in favour of forced paper currency. Pieces of locally stamped paper are, it is averred, quite sufficient for purposes of local circulation. The absurdity of attempting by legislation to endow intrinsically worthless pieces of rag (which are *not* promises to pay on demand in coin) with a nominal value has but too often been made apparent. From the American "greenback" to the Argentine "shin plaster" the results of such forced currencies have always been the same—ruinous alike to credit and to Trade.

END OF APPENDIX.

PART II.

THE
TRADE ECONOMY OF FEDERATION.

THE TRADE ECONOMY OF FEDERATION.

THE political aspects of Federation lie beyond the scope of the present inquiry, which is based essentially upon Economic considerations; and, although it is difficult to conceive a commercial union which would not also be to a great extent political, the fact is daily becoming more evident that the former must precede the latter. It is true that those who may be termed Political Federationists are not yet generally prepared to admit this; that many able advocates still contend that political union should come first. But the weight of evidence is against them; nor do they appear to realise that Mammon is a far stronger stimulus than patriotism to all sections of the British race. Political arguments are based chiefly upon sentiment; they have been tried, and found wanting. Economic arguments are based entirely upon profit and loss, and are far more likely to succeed.

It has been shown that Free Trade is a radically sound policy, and that Protection is radically unsound. And it has been shown that possible expediency, based upon causes underlying national existence, is the one solitary argument that can ever justify a Protectionist policy. Upon these two principles the entire science of Trade Economy is based. Unfortunately, however, the Cobden-Bright school of Economists, the founders of England's commercial policy, did not recognise the second of these principles as a principle at all. With them (as still with their followers) Protection was a rank heresy foredoomed to be swept away before the true faith of Free Trade. It was part of the faith that was in them; they predicted from every platform that foreign nations would speedily be converted from the error of their ways and follow England's example. *Magna est veritas et prævalebit*, was their text. To convert Englishmen by a promise of a "cheap loaf" was an easy task; and Sir Robert Peel and Parliament, of course, followed suit. But the conversion of the foreigners was left to time, and regarded as a matter of course. Cobden lived long enough to see Free Trade England's accepted policy, the cheap loaf an accomplished fact, and her industries increasing with enormous strides. He died a staunch Free Trader, regretting only that he could not live to see Protection extirpated. Bright died a generation later, not having seen the prophecy fulfilled, and also a Free Trader to the last. He bewailed the perverse obstinacy of foreign nations, but (such is the obstinacy of enthusiasm) he neither understood its *cause*, nor rightly estimated its *powers of endurance*. Neither do the vast majority of Free Traders at the present time. Hence, it is of the very utmost importance to inquire most carefully into these two points.

Why Foreign Nations are Protectionist.

Great Britain is marked out by Nature as the workshop of the world. She has vast deposits of coal and iron lying side by side, and these are the very basis of manufacturing enterprise. Geographically, she occupies the centre of the land-surface of the earth. Her insular position not only affords her an immunity from attack, which has made it possible for her alone of European nations to dispense with the withering curse of military conscription, but, furthermore, gives her absolutely unrivalled shipping facilities. She had a long start in the industrial race by her inventions of steam and labour-saving machinery. Her vast accumulation of capital, the numbers, energy, and skill of her operatives, have enabled her to reduce the costs of manufactures to a point against which no foreigner can compete in an open market. Omitting the United States (whose reasons for adopting a Protective policy have already been clearly shown), what other nation possesses even a small fraction of

Great Britain's manufacturing advantages? And, moreover, they are crippled by the necessity of having to withdraw the very flower of their manhood from productive employment in order to keep up millions of productively idle troops. Suppose, now, that foreign nations had followed England's example, and had thrown open their ports and frontier-customs. What would have been the inevitable result upon their native industries? More or less rapid extinction in manufactures, and diminished distribution in raw produce. It is true that such extinction of costly manufactures and such diminution of costly distribution would both be productive gains from a social-scientific point of view, and that labour would thereby be forced into more profitable channels. But social science does not assert that the displaced labour would necessarily find such new profitable channels in any one country. If, for example, the silk industries of Lyons or the textile factories of Silesia ceased to exist, Lyonese and Silesian operatives would not necessarily find other employment in France and Germany. They would far more probably, and, certainly, more wisely, follow their trades abroad. And if this consideration be extended to entire populations, the conclusions are startling. In Germany, 43 per cent. of the population live by agriculture, 10 per cent. by commerce and the carrying Trade, and the balance, 47 per cent., by Protected industries, *i.e.*, by industries which would collapse were Protection withdrawn; else, why protect them? In France, the proportions are nearly the same. In both countries, the industrial centres are gaining at the expense of the agricultural districts. Germany has, however, this advantage, that whereas her population is increasing rapidly, that of France is almost at a standstill. What, now, would be the result to either country of a reversal of the Protectionist policy? Evidently a redistribution of, roughly, one-half the existing labour, and, mainly, into agricultural or raw-producing channels. But, in the first place, raw production could not stand such an enormous accession to its ranks. And, in the second place, it is a well-established fact that, although the yokel takes readily and kindly to town-life, the artisan has an utter abhorrence of agricultural labour. Consequently, the outcome would be a rapid loss of population, with prospects of but a slow subsequent re-increase, a heavy loss in revenue, and a perilous diminution of the national armies. Finally, if the now Protected industries disappeared, and each nation were left at the mercy of foreign supplies, what would happen in the at-all-times probable event of war? Englishmen should strive to disabuse themselves of the Cobdenite notion that foreign statesmen and

Economists are foolishly infatuated with Protection. They see, they have seen all along, the great advantages of Free Trade—to England. But they see also the expediency of, nay, the absolute necessity for Protection—to themselves. And, until the existing European bayonet-policy undergoes a radical change, until Tennyson's grand lines are realised, it is as futile as it is unreasonable to look for any alteration in Continental Trade policy.

Such being the cause, which Cobden and Free Traders have entirely overlooked, let us now glance at the second point, which they have just as entirely underrated.

Protectionist Powers of Endurance.

If the reader will be at the pains of referring to an appendix note upon Foreign Trade, he will observe that Protected countries have small trade-averages. As a natural corollary to taxing imports, they have had to frame their production policy upon the lines of dispensing with foreign products, so far as they possibly could. These lines were terribly expensive, especially at first; but they had to bear them. They have been expensive throughout; but still they have borne them. Custom is a second nature. The longer foreign communities taxed their own pockets by taxing imports, the more they got used to the tax; until finally artificially-enhanced prices came to be popularly accepted as fair values. In the case of the vast majority of such communities, foreign trade has gradually come down so as to figure as but a subsidiary item in the national accounts. Their trade tends to become and, in course of time, does become an internal or local trade. Their surplus produce they export for just what it may chance to fetch, and receive, in return, commodities which either they absolutely cannot themselves produce, or of which they may happen to be short. This sort of traffic bears about the same relationship to legitimate commerce, as does a draper's "Annual Sale at an Alarming Sacrifice" to his legitimate business. Because, forsooth, England has become dependent upon *her* foreign trade for the very bread she eats, it has been taken for granted that other nations would similarly become dependent, if not for food, at least for other necessaries, upon *their* foreign trade. This assumption has not been borne out by the results of some forty years of Free Trade experience. If England, by a sudden convulsion of nature, were suddenly to disappear from the face of the earth, foreigners would still contrive to wear clothes, whereas, were she spared and they engulfed, cannibalism would be rampant in England within six weeks. It is not to be inferred that, because foreign policy tends to destroy foreign trade, therefore foreign commercial men despise it. On the contrary, they labour hard to keep as much of it as they can, and are very pushing with their surplus produce. So, too, our friend, the draper, makes the most of his clearing sale. But what can they do against the Protectionist will and the Protectionist laws of a nation? Merely emphasise the fact, in figures, that Protection aims at reducing foreign trade to a minimum. And this is why Free Traders have been waiting in vain for signs of decay in Protective policy.

Why Protection is Increasing.

Well, simply because it has failed, so far, in accomplishing the object for which it was adopted, *viz.* the Protection of native industries from foreign (chiefly British) competition. It is easily understood that tariffs are necessarily tentative and elastic. The British manufacturer has hitherto contrived, by using improved machinery and by taking full advantage of a cheap and overcrowded labour market, to reduce the expenses of manufacture; and so, in spite of tariffs, to compete, upon something like fair terms, with foreign producers. (The reason why these tariffs were not long ago made absolutely prohibitive will appear in the next section.) Moreover, he has many times engaged, and undersold foreigners, in special lines which, it had been thought, were safe from his competition. These have had to, and still have to, be added to the list. Nothing is safe from him. He can, if he gets but half a chance, successfully imitate and undersell anything and everything. Hence clamours continually arise for more extended and more severe import duties; and to these clamours Protectionist Governments respond willingly enough. No other course is, indeed, logically open to them.

They cannot, fairly, favour one set of producers more than another. And it is evidently no use imposing duties at all, if these duties fail in their effects. Consequently Protection has been, and still is, steadily increasing in intensity and in extent. This fact is so notorious in English commercial circles, and so frequently referred to in the daily press, that it is quite unnecessary to support it by special quotation from, or reference to, such measures as the M'Kinley tariff or the later additions to Continental tariffs.

How England has Hitherto Evaded Prohibitive Tariffs.

It is obvious that were foreign markets protected all round by absolutely prohibitive tariffs, foreign trade would cease altogether. And the fact that England has been doing three-fourths of her total trade with foreign nations, is plain proof that, up to the present, their tariffs have not been prohibitive, but, rather, more or less moderate encouragements to local industries, viewed as a convenient method of raising revenue by indirect taxation. Yet this moderation runs directly counter to the expedient policy of these nations. How, then, has England managed to secure such favourable treatment? The answer is, it must be confessed, more creditable to English smartness than to English justice. She has, throughout, persuaded foreign Governments to relax rigid Protection in her favour by offering them, in return, that which is not hers to give—special advantages in the markets of her (avowedly) self-governing Colonies. She has, at various times, made such treaties as the following, in every one of which she has coolly mortgaged the commercial freedom of every single dependency of the British Crown; and, in exchange, she has been admitted by these foreign

Governments to the specially lenient tariff treatment provided by "most-favoured nation" clauses.

Treaty with	Expires	Sample Clauses.
France	Feb. 1st, 1892	"The produce or manufacture of Belgium shall not be subject in the British Colonies to other or higher duties than those which are or may be imposed upon similar articles of British origin."—*Treaty with Belgium, July 23rd, 1862*
Italy	Feb. 1st, 1892	
Spain	March, 1892	
Portugal	June, 1892	
Bulgaria	August, 1892	
Roumania	July, 1892	
Germany }		"In the Colonies and Possessions of Her Britannic Majesty the produce of the State of the Zollverein shall not be subject to any higher or other import duties than the produce of the United Kingdom of Great Britain and Ireland."—*Treaty with German Zollverein, May 30th, 1865.*
Russia		
Holland		
Belgium	At one year's notice on either side.	
Sweden		
Norway		
Denmark		
Switzerland		
Austria-Hungary		

This is bad enough; but it is not all. By an additional stretch of Imperial authority, these clauses were so interpreted as to debar the Colonies from even making special commercial agreements with each other! Thus several of the Australian Colonies would gladly have made differential tariff[1] arrange-

---

[1] "Differential" tariffs are modifications of the existing protective duties of a country in favour of one or more other countries, with respect to certain commodities. The terms "reciprocal" and "reciprocity" should, strictly, be reserved to

ments with Canada, but it was found to be impossible, owing to England's treaties, without admitting the whole world, well-nigh, to the benefits of the compact. Naturally the Colonies have protested against such arbitrary and high-handed procedure, and probably most Englishmen will admit that they have good cause for complaint. And as it will be seen from the table given that some of these treaties will expire at various dates this year, the question of their renewal will shortly form a leading Economic point. Of course if England were to insist upon such renewal, she could do so at the risk of a serious quarrel with her Dependencies. Whilst, upon the other hand, if she does not renew them, how is she to secure "most-favoured nation" privileges for her produce? Is a hungry man justified in selling his children's clothes to buy bread for himself? The question is one which Englishmen will, later on, be called upon to decide; and it is distinctly a very awkward one.

The reader will here, very probably, exclaim, "Then, after all, it is not unassisted Free Trade which has carried England through, all these years! So far from Free Trade combating Protection upon

denote exact similarity, or absence of tariffs between countries together with similar protective duties against other countries. But "differential" and "reciprocal," as commonly used, are well-nigh interchangeable terms.

its own merits, it has been bribing its way into Protected markets!" Well, it certainly does not seem to bear out the Cobdenite theory that England *alone* would uproot Protection. But more than this I do not care to say; firstly, because I am myself a Colonial; and, secondly, because it lies rather within my province to enable the reader to form intelligent opinions of his own than to give him mine.

It should here be noted that there is a possibility of the foreign Governments refusing to renew the treaties upon the old terms, as well as of England anticipating such refusal; in which case England's action might depend upon the nature of any fresh conditions proposed; whilst, of course, a point-blank refusal, by either side, to renew upon any terms, would at once bring matters to a climax. So far there is evidence only to show that most of the foreign Governments are raising, or preparing to raise, their tariffs, that the London Board of Trade and Chamber of Commerce are cautiously feeling their way, and that the Colonies will use every possible effort to have the treaties torn up. Not at all impossibly, some proposal may by-and-bye be agreed to, to renew the treaties, upon the present lines, for a fixed period, so as to afford full time for discussion and avert a very serious commercial crisis. But it is always wise to be prepared for the worst, and

Englishmen should, whilst there is yet ample time, accustom themselves to reflecting upon the immediate effects which the repudiation of those treaties would have upon England's Trade. And these may, with tolerable certainty, be foreshadowed. The one restraining cause once gone, of course there would remain nothing wherewith to purchase entry into Protected ports.

So soon as tariffs were raised to the prohibitive point, England would be commercially ostracised, and her Trade with foreign nations a thing of the past.

There would remain the Colonies and Dependencies. But they, with here and there an exception, are also highly Protectionist, and would certainly not throw open their ports out of any sentimental regard for the mother country which has, all these years, been sacrificing their commercial freedom to appease her foreign customers. She cannot *force* them to admit her goods upon her own terms. What could she do? Evidently, under the supposed conditions, there would be but one course left to her—Trade with them upon such terms as they might be willing to agree to; or, in other words, enter with them into a Britannic Commercial Federation.

That is the form into which coming events seem best fitted to be shaped, if only a wise foresight be used in directing them. I have read somewhere, in this connection, that "events are wiser than men." But this appears to me to be rank fatalism, or still ranker nonsense. Most certainly social science seeks to guide the sequence of foreseen events, not to act, upon the spur of the moment, as they happen. And considering that the existence of prohibitive foreign tariffs and the disappearance of the treaties are both, at the utmost, merely a matter of time, the engrossing question of interest to all British social scientists must surely be the elaboration of a commercial union upon the existence of which the future of England's commerce must entirely depend. In which spirit, I venture to contribute my mite towards a successful issue.

So many, so various, and so important are the considerations involved, that it is not easy to decide in what order they should be dealt with. The sequence which I have followed seems to cover most of the ground in broad outline; though, of course, the side issues are innumerable.

I. Should the proposed Commercial Union be rigidly confined to communities owing allegiance to the British Crown?

Yes. It is impossible to admit *foreign* communities to a *Britannic* Union, which must eventually be followed by a political Britannic Confederation. But it is by no means impossible to admit such of them, as may ask to be admitted, to a Britannic Commercial Alliance. Indeed, a little reflection will make it appear that the concession of such an Alliance would be as clearly a matter of justice as of expediency.

It would be grossly unfair to ostracise a large number of small nations, which, at present, are Protectionist chiefly for the sake of revenue, without giving them a chance of repentance. And, moreover, a door should always be left open even for the greater nations (which, as a matter of course, will sulk at first and, perhaps, for a very long time) should they eventually decide to lower their tariffs.

The amount of British capital at present invested abroad in all sorts of securities and enterprises, good, dubious, and rotten, would challenge belief were it added up and set down in hundreds of millions of pounds sterling. I have neither leisure nor available statistics for exact inquiry upon this point; but I may cite one example. The Argentine Republic has absorbed in debt, railways, and industrial enterprises generally, certainly not less than £200,000,000, of which fully two-thirds are British investments. Roughly speaking, there cannot be less than £590,000,000 of British capital invested outside the limits of the British Empire. And I need scarcely point out that this enormous sum must be commercially safeguarded so far as may be possible.

II. Upon what terms should alien nations be admissible?

Under a Britannic Commercial Alliance Treaty embodying differential tariffs with the Britannic Commercial Union. The just principle should prevail, not to exclude foreigners simply because they are foreigners, but to admit them, if they choose to enter, upon terms of reciprocity. More detailed suggestions will appear in a later section.

III. Can any estimate be formed as to what nations would probably join such an Alliance?

In all probability, those nations which are at present most *dependent* upon British Trade for their supplies and for their revenues, and to which a foreign Trade is of more importance than considerations of purely national policy. In which category the following nine nations, which are, at present, England's best foreign customers, would *not* be found.[1]

---

[1] Italy is not included among outside nations because she is regarded as certain to join the Union in Alliance. Probabilities point in the same direction in the case of Sweden, Norway, Denmark, Turkey, and Greece.

	Trade with Great Britain (1889).
United States	£139,340,409
France	67,881,499
Germany	58,249,563
Holland	42,863,002
Russia	35,797,746
Belgium	31,284,452
Spain	16,466,751
Portugal	6,097,037
Roumania	4,513,598
	£402,454,057

These nations, with the smaller States more or less dependent upon them, would, in fact, be the upholders of rigid, isolated Protection. The rest of the world would trade within the sphere of the Britannic Commercial Union, or of the Britannic Commercial Alliance.

IV. In what position would British Trade then be as compared with what it is now?

Practically, it is impossible that Trade should wholly cease between the Union and the countries enumerated above, which may be termed "outside nations." Some fraction of trade would inevitably survive even the most drastic Protective tariffs. But let us ignore this fraction (which, of course, would be upon the credit side) and suppose the very worst, *viz.* that Trade entirely ceased between the outside nations and the Union. We must then deduct the present amount of their Trade, and then see how far the deficiency could be made good from fresh sources. The entire volume of Colonial Trade would be kept within the Union; and allowance must be made for increased Alliance Trade. The profit and loss account would appear to stand thus:

OLD ACCOUNT.

Great Britain's Trade with the nine countries named	£402,454,057
,, ,, British Colonies, etc.	187,695,862
,, ,, other nations	152,213,217
	£742,363,136

NEW ACCOUNT.

Total Trade of British Colonies, etc. (1889)	£431,637,864
Trade of other nations (Alliance)	152,213,217
Estimated increase under Alliance	50,000,000
	£633,851,081

This means that the entire Trade of the Union would be £108,512,055 less than that of Great Britain alone now is; or £540,248,919 less than the whole Trade of the British Empire is at present. If, indeed, Great Britain could secure the whole of the new Colonial Trade, the prospect would not be so serious. But she cannot; it is unreasonable to credit her with more than two-thirds of it. And, thus, her individual Trade would sink to £489,971,793, a decrease of £252,391,343 upon existing figures.

This is by no means synonymous with national ruin. Far from it. But it is certainly synonymous with very serious national loss, and may well impress all with a sense of the gravity of the situation during the next few years. Still we must never lose sight of the far more overwhelming disasters that would be in store for us had we no Colonial Empire to fall back upon; for, plainly, had we no materials wherewith to build up a Commercial Union of our own, we would lie wholly at the mercy of prohibitive foreign tariffs. Nor must we overlook the fact that it will be mainly with Great Britain to minimise her threatened losses by concentrating her energy and her capital upon the unlimited industrial resources of her dominions. In our estimate we have made no allowance for Colonial Trade expansion. Yet there is no reason, as will presently be shown, why such expansion should not take place, and to the extent of wiping out the Trade deficit within a reasonably short period.

V. Upon what basis is it probable that a Britannic Commercial Union could be formed?

Staunch Free Traders will here at once rush into the breach and exclaim, "Free Trade amongst all component States of the Union, with reciprocal or differential tariffs against the rest of the world!" Impossible. The Colonies would simply refuse to listen to such a proposal, and, without their co-operation, of course no Union is possible. It has been shown, in an earlier portion of this work, that national expediency is the mainspring of Protection, the one sound argument upon which it is based. But, as there is a very general belief, in England, that the Colonies adopt a Protective policy chiefly for revenue purposes, this is an opportune moment to prove that this belief is quite erroneous, that revenue-raising is merely a secondary consideration. In order to do this, I propose to compare two Colonies, Victoria and New South Wales, which pursue totally different systems of Trade policy.

	Policy.	Population.	Trade.	Revenue.
Victoria	Protection	1,104,288	£37,825,897	£8,674,710
New South Wales	Free Trade	1,122,200	46,157,991	9,063,397

It is true that New South Wales has a larger area than her sister Colony, but (as has many times been statistically proved by the New South Wales Free Trade Association) if the land revenues of both be set aside, the balance is still heavily in favour of New South Wales. Here, then, we have clear evidence that tariff imposts are neither necessary nor profitable from a revenue aspect. They are, indeed, avowedly resorted to "to protect native industries," as is implied by the very name, "Protection;" or, in other words, they are, by all the Colonies, except New South Wales, deemed to be nationally expedient And nothing having occurred, or having been authoritatively suggested, so far, to cause the Colonies to alter their views as to national expediency, it is useless even to hint at Free Trade to them. To clench the matter, as it were, it may be noted that an Australian National Convention met in Sydney, in March 1891, for three principal objects: to federate the Australian Colonies, to discuss Great Britain's foreign treaties, and to arrange inter-colonial differential tariffs, New South Wales being in a minority of 1 to 5.

We have next to consider whether it would be possible to leave each State in the proposed Union perfectly free to regulate its own tariffs as regards other States and nations in commercial alliance. No; this could not be. There must be some tariff limit. Otherwise the threatened European tariff deadlock would be continually cropping up, on a smaller scale, within the Union; separate little differential Unions would be formed; and the trouble would be perpetuated. Moreover, if there be not unity of Trade policy, how can there be a Commercial Union at all?

VI. How, then, is it possible to reconcile English

Free Trade requirements with Colonial Protective insistence?

By *compromise*. England must modify the Free Trade taught by Cobden, and the Colonies must modify the Protective tariffs taught by expediency. *In medio tutissimus ibis:* the difficulty is to plan out a safe middle course. That the problem can and will be solved, in time and after due discussion, may, I hope, be regarded as certain; but it will tax all that there is of brain-power and of statesmanship in the Empire to solve it. The public mind must be aroused in every section of our dominions to a just appreciation of the tremendous issues at stake. The question must be viewed as a national one, and must be so discussed alike in every senate and in every village debating club. Trade conferences must be held, in order that the special interests of every community may be clearly set forth and none be overlooked or neglected. The press, that mighty mirror of national opinion, must devote its trained critical power to sifting the grain of practicability from the chaff of ill-considered proposals. Each one of us may do something towards a solution, though no one of us may be able to do much. And having thought out an opinion, it becomes the duty of each to formulate it, in order that its value may be recognised or its worthlessness exposed.

VII. Suggestions for a basis.

Economic distribution of production must be studied.
No Commercial Union could be effected upon a basis of enabling each community to become its own "universal provider." Upon the other hand, no one nation can be allowed a manufacturing monopoly of everything. Hence it is necessary to distinguish, in the case of each community, between its naturally most advantageous and its naturally least advantageous lines of production. Now, no country imports that which it can profitably produce, nor exports that which the purchasing country, or countries, can profitably produce. Therefore a country's imports are an index to its productive weakness, and its exports an index to its productive strength. Hitherto manufacturing Free Trade has advised, " Devote all your energies to your exports, *I* will supply you with imports." Whereto raw-producing Protection has replied, " Our strong lines of production, our exports, are very well able to look after themselves; but our weak lines, as shown by our imports, need to be protected." Wherein lies the safe middle course between these extremes of policy? Clearly a distinction must first be drawn between imports of prime and imports of secondary importance; between, for example, necessary wearing apparel and fancy biscuits. For the former the term "staple," and for the latter,

"secondary," might conveniently be adopted. The import returns of each community would show which are its principal staple, and which its most valuable secondary imports, the line of demarcation being arbitrarily, but easily, fixed. Then, with respect to both categories, the argument would hold good that large importation of particular commodities proves at once their indispensability to the community, and the extreme difficulty or impossibility of producing them locally; but only in the case of staples need the argument be pressed to its logical conclusion. That conclusion, of course, is that such staples should be very lightly taxed (if taxed at all) *quoad* other States of the Union, more highly taxed *quoad* States in Alliance, and prohibitively taxed *quoad* outside nations. If, for example, woollens are a staple Canadian import, in spite of existing tariffs, the attempt to foster woollen industries in Canada is evidently a failure. Yet they are of necessity to the Canadian people. Remove, therefore, the tax upon woollens. This, it will be seen, is a great concession to Free Trade principles. Upon the other hand, those staples which are least imported, but are, at the same time, largely consumed, point to the conclusion that they have, as industries, taken strong, healthy root locally under Protection tariffs, and have thereby justified their claim to continued Protection. For instance, I can buy a locally-made tweed in Geelong (Victoria), or in Mosgiel (New Zealand), as good in quality and nearly as cheap as in Bradford, which proves that this particular industry has been successfully Protected. Therefore, in the case of these two Colonies, by all means maintain the tariff upon tweeds. And this is an equally great concession to Protectionist principles.

As regards the least important staples and the secondary imports, there does not appear to be any necessity to protest against the right of each State to fix its own tariffs within some reasonable limit agreed to by all; but, still, with a higher tariff for States in Alliance, and prohibition for outside nations. In practice, the acceptance of such a basis would necessitate considerable revision of existing tariffs, and would result in great diversity of tariffs throughout the Empire. But the former change would really involve little more than clerical work; whilst the latter would be distinctly beneficial to the shipping interests. There would inevitably be complaints from those who, under uneconomically-devised tariffs, have embarked in enterprises utterly uncongenial to local capabilities. But that cannot be helped; the interests of the consuming majority must come before those of the ill-advised, dear-producing minority. And it will be allowed that, from an economic distribution point of view, the suggestion goes almost as far as possible towards reconciling the conflicting interests of Free Trade and Protection.

Raw imports must be Protected as well as manufactured goods. That is to say, England must Protect Colonial raw produce against competition from alien nations, though, as before, with a discrimination between nations in alliance and outside nations. This is a *sine quâ non;* because otherwise the Colonies would reap no benefit whatever from the Union. For example, Australian wool must be Protected against South American wool, so as to give it a distinct advantage; whilst against Continental or American wool, it must be rigidly safeguarded. Wool may not appear to be a very happily chosen illustration, since the Australian and Cape Colonies have almost a monopoly in its production. But that is not the point. Foreign nations outside the Alliance must find no market for their produce, raw or manufactured, within the British Empire. This is the very *raison d'être* of the Commercial Union. If any attempt be made to discriminate between imports and exports, or between raw and manufactured produce in favour of outside nations, the Colonies, seeing no *quid pro quo*, will have nothing to do with a Union at all. It is just possible that they would consent to make an exception for a definite number of years in the case of one great English staple import—cotton, and upon the following grounds: none of the Colonies produce it; it is a necessary of everyday life; and it would be unfair to crush suddenly the enormous English interests vested in its manufacture. India and Egypt would suffer most by England's retention of the American supply; but a small differential tariff in their favour would, perhaps, stimulate them to overtake America within, say, ten years. In point of fact, they are coming up reasonably fast already, considering how short a time they have been cotton-growing.

It may here be remarked that although the United States exported to England in 1889, £33,811,444 worth of raw cotton, they only took back £2,306,600 worth of English cotton manufactures; and the M'Kinley tariff has now made even this beggarly export of English goods impossible! Does it not seem hard that we should have to buy their raw material until India and Egypt can supply us? But social science is above all feelings of retaliation—unless it pays.

Moreover, although, upon the whole, by far the larger portion of England's trade is, as we have seen, with foreign nations, yet her own diminions are, proportionately, by far her best purchasing customers.

The Trade Economy of Federation. 121

British imports from foreign countries	£330,371,524
British exports to foreign countries	224,275,950
Excess of imports	£106,095,574
British imports from Colonies, etc.	£97,266,071
British exports to Colonies, etc.	90,429,791
Excess of imports	£6,836,280

As samples of important imports (other than food), which England at present receives from the Colonies, the following percentages, compiled from Board of Trade returns for year ending November, 1890, may be quoted:—

	Percentage received from Colonies, etc.
Wool	90 per cent.
Tallow	50 ,,
Leather	41 ,,
Cotton	23 ,,
Tin	92 ,,
Copper	32 ,,

Whilst of manufactures exported by England, the following headings (representing about 42 per cent. of the entire Colonial import Trade from England, and about 17 per cent. of the entire import foreign

Trade from England) show some lines wherein the Colonies rather more than hold their own :—

Manufactures exported by Great Britain to:

British Colonies, etc.		Foreign Nations.
Cotton	£22,795,014	£26,435,986
Wearing Apparel	3,754,296	866,200
Haberdashery	1,423,297	533,318
Boots and Shoes	1,286,013	429,762
Woollen tissues	1,216,768	1,710,565
Railroads, etc.	3,630,288	3,403,453
Cutlery	1,050,870	1,390,126
Paper	805,065	295,725
Beer	1,001,099	665,411
Spirits	1,066,924	235,163
	£38,029,634	£35,575,709

VIII. Great Britain's Food Supply.

Could Great Britain's enormous and steadily increasing requirements in the shape of food be adequately met by the proposed Commercial Union?

This will by many be regarded as the most important question of all. England, it will be urged, might survive loss in her Trade, and might even do so with some show of cheerfulness, if it be made clear that such loss will only be temporary. But food she must have, even had she to go down upon her knees, metaphorically, to her foreign customers, and put up with the very worst they can do in the way of tariff persecution. Therefore, much as such a Commercial Union is to be desired, and brilliant as are the prospects which it opens out, so long as Englishmen are dependent upon the foreigner for the very bread they eat, it is a dream impossible of realisation.

The contention is a just one; but, after all, it begs the question. That England, at the present time, receives by far the greater proportion of her imported food from alien sources, will be evident from a few items of important products—the absolute necessaries, we may say, of subsistence.

	From Colonies, etc.	From Foreign Countries.
Wheat, corn, etc.,	24 per cent.	76 per cent.
Flour,	12 ,,	88 ,,
Live cattle,	22 ,,	78 ,,
Dead cattle,	31 ,,	69 ,,
Fresh mutton,	49 ,,	51 ,,
Sugar,	16 ,,	84 ,,
Tea,	72 ,,	28 ,,
Coffee,	37 ,,	63 ,,
Rice,	80 ,,	20 ,,

Or, taking a general average of these articles, England imports 38·1 per cent. from her own possessions, and 61·9 per cent. from alien countries. The nature and value of her food imports for the past year were as follows;

Live Animals.	Meat, Butter, Cheese and Eggs.	Wheat and Flour.	Grain and Sugar.	Fruit and Vegetables.	Totals.
£	£	£	£	£	£
10,359,852	45,355,581	31,054,410	47,365,135	6,884,787	141,019,765

Not wishing to overload this work with statistics, I refrain from showing the source of each and every one of these items. It is necessary, however, to state that, taking the whole of the food imports, the British possessions do not show even 38 per cent., emerging with 32·7 or, say, one-third. They receive, consequently, £47,006,588, as against £94,013,177 received by foreign nations for food supplies. And it is clear that England at present cannot dispense with the foreigner.

But, if it can further be shown that her present dependence upon alien sources is entirely her own fault, and that her own possessions could easily be made to take the foreigner's place, this apparently strong objection to the Commercial Union will be overcome.

That it is her own fault is but another way of saying that it is the inevitable outcome of her past Trade policy of sacrificing her Colonial to her foreign commerce; and this (treaties included) has, I hope, been abundantly proved already.

As to the powers of the British possessions to

treble the amount of their present food contributions, *that* demands a very careful economic consideration both of the products required, and of the advantages existing in various sections of the Empire for their production.

Live Animals: Cattle. The number imported fluctuates extraordinarily from year to year. Thus, it was 474,750 in 1883; 295,961 in 1887; and 555,222 in 1889, of which latter number, 126,000 came from Canada. Could Canada supply the whole demand? Not quite, for a few years to come, since there are in the whole of British North America but 2,391,000 head; but with a little tariff encouragement she could considerably increase her present export. Australia (*with her* 11,412,986 *cattle*) is too far for the live traffic. If, however, a couple of the South American republics, Argentina and Uruguay, came into Alliance (as they to a certainty would), the balance could easily be made up. Between them they own nearly 23,000,000 head, accepting local statistics. Within the last few months I have myself returned from a lengthy visit to the River Plate, and can certify, from personal up-country experience, that practically unlimited droves of fairly fat *novillos* (four-year-old steers) may be bought at from fourteen to eighteen shillings a-piece. Moreover, a large and increasing traffic has sprung up in live sheep between Buenos

Ayres, Montevideo, and Liverpool. If it pays to carry sheep, why not cattle also? This is, of course, a question for experts in the cattle trade to answer. But even if their answer be unfavourable, there is still the frozen beef to fall back upon; and of this the supply is literally inexhaustible. Why, Queensland alone, with her 5,000,000 head of cattle, and the numerous refrigerating works erected at Brisbane, Rockhampton, etc., in anticipation of orders which have not yet arrived, could supply the English markets abundantly—to say nothing of all the other Colonies.

Live animals: Sheep. The live sheep trade fluctuates even more than that in cattle. As long ago as 1882 1,124,391 were imported, whereas in 1889 the number fell to 677,958, a decline probably largely due to increase in the frozen mutton trade, especially with New Zealand. The new live sheep trade with the River Plate will certainly bring up the numbers again for 1890; and Argentina claims to have the enormous number of 84,000,000 sheep to draw upon. The numbers in Australia are still larger, reaching the marvellous total of 101,000,000! Surely with the resources of the Cape, Canada, and the other possessions thrown in, the prospect of dear mutton, at all events, seems invisible.

In connection with the frozen meat trade, it may

be remarked, that the popular prejudice against it is rapidly dying out; indeed, thousands eat it daily without knowing it. And, furthermore, that there exists a strong ring of middlemen for the purpose of keeping up retail prices. It is an economic fact, which has been demonstrated over and over again, that frozen mutton *should not* cost more than 2½d. to 3d. per lb. retail; beef should average 1d. to 1½d. more per lb. Co-operation is needed here.

Live animals: Pigs. The number imported in 1889 was 25,324, and, seeing that there are 835,469 in Ontario and Quebec alone, fresh pork can never become scarce.

As for the various sorts of meat, other than live and frozen, the figures already quoted prove conclusively that there is no occasion to apply to the united States, or to the Continent, for a single mouthful. And be it carefully observed that we have, so far, had no occasion to go beyond two of our Colonies, with the alternative co-operation of a couple of States in Alliance.

Prices would not be sensibly affected, because the meat resources at our command are so vast that the keenest competition would set in once the foreigner was excluded by a moderate tariff against him.

Butter, Cheese, and Eggs. For fresh butter and eggs, England would have to look mainly to herself and to Canada. And, upon sound economic grounds, it would vastly improve the condition of her own rural districts, were she so compelled to look. Economists have for years been preaching to unheeding British farmers the expediency of devoting themselves to dairy-produce, poultry, and vegetables. But the British farmer is conservative and ultra-slow in grasping new ideas. He hankers after the plough, and he dislikes the spade; he despises the milk-pail, and he loathes the hen-roost. He wants to do as his father did before the corn laws came into existence; but he can't. Wheat and cereals of all kinds can now be grown in the Antipodes and placed upon the London market at a price with which he cannot compete. If he *will* be a ploughman, he must migrate to the Colonies and take his plough with him. In England, with his ideas, he is an anachronism, a glaring instance of the wide-spread ignorance of profitable distribution pointed out in an earlier portion of this work. As an agriculturist, *he* cannot hope to benefit by any tariff against foreign cereals, since it is not proposed to protect him against British possessions; and this fact I desire especially to impress upon country readers. Dairy-farming has, of late years, made considerable progress. It must make still more; and to it must be superadded poultry-farming and market-gardening. Canada can greatly increase her output; but she will not, for very many years, be able to meet the present large demand. There is therefore every encouragement for the British rural populations to engage in these industries, in which (another great advantage) a woman's labour very nearly equals a man's. Failing such awakening to modern exigencies, it is useless blinking our eyes to the certainty that fresh butter and eggs will, in a few years at most, be scarce and dear.

Salted butter and cheese need occasion no anxiety, since they can travel any distance. At present this industry is shamefully neglected in Australia, simply because, with all their vast herds, it does not pay to export against American and Continental competition; and Australians themselves care little for dairy produce. Highly sweetened tea without milk is the ordinary national beverage.

Wheat and Flour. Here we stand upon especially firm ground. Whatever excuses her apologists may find for England in the matter of the foreign treaties (and they certainly are not very apparent), there are absolutely none for her blind, unreasoning Cobdenism in the matter of bread-stuffs, because ignorance of the wheat-producing capabilities of her own dominions is a stain upon English statesmanship, not an excuse. She has literally built up American agricultural in-

I

terests. Her capitalists supplied the means of starting the vast wheat farms, and of constructing the railways for conveyance of the produce to British ships for carriage to English markets. Her surplus population has streamed in millions towards the favoured Republic. All for what? In order that ministers might be able to boast about the famous "cheap loaf." Has it been a cheap loaf? No; unless all our arguments against Protection are worthless; it must have been a dear loaf, for the simple reason that *everything* in a Protected country is produced at a maximum cost. It is quite true that it has been, at all events, the cheapest loaf which the world offered for sale. It is quite true also that the principles of Free Trade teach us to buy in the cheapest market. Yes; but Free Trade, or, at least, intelligent Free Trade, does not teach us to bolster up foreign Protectionist industries, and then try to persuade ourselves that we have done the best we could. However, a few figures will soon clear up this point. I have taken prices during the ten years preceding the Corn Bill, and also during the same period afterwards, and I have averaged both. There is a difference in the two periods of 1s. 1d. It may be urged that this difference would have been greater but for the Crimean War. So, too, it might have been less, but for the bad harvests that followed Her Majesty's accession. I have added prices and average during the past ten years.

Average price of Wheat before and after the Corn Bill of 1846:

	Per Quarter.				Per Quarter.	
	S.	D.			S.	D.
1835	39	4		1846	54	8
1836	48	6		1847	69	9
1837	55	10		1848	50	6
1838	64	7		1849	44	3
1839	70	8		1850	40	3
1840	66	4		1851	38	6
1841	64	4		1852	40	9
1842	57	3		1853	52	3
1843	50	1		1854	72	5
1844	51	3		1855	74	8
1845	50	10		1856	69	2
	11 | 619	0			11 | 607	2
Average : 56·27s.				Average : 55·19s.		

Or, 56s. 3d. nearly.   Or, 55s. 2d. nearly.

Prices and average during the past ten years:

	Per Quarter.				Per Quarter.	
	S.	D.			S.	D.
1880	44	4		1885	32	10
1881	45	4		1886	31	0
1882	45	1		1887	32	6
1883	41	7		1888	31	10
1884	35	8		1889	29	9
					10 | 369	11
				Average : 37s. nearly.		

After all, then, wheat has, in spite of fluctuations, fallen in price since 1846, when Sir Robert Peel passed his Corn Bill and gladdened the souls of all good Cobdenites. Yes; and I have no quarrel with Sir Robert Peel's Bill, but only with the cosmopolitan Cobdenism that could not see its way to taking a statesmanlike view of the inevitable ultimate effects of that Act: that had a nose to sniff out the means of cheapening bread, but could not see a yard ahead of that nose. In the ordinary course of events, as knowledge of scientific farming extended, and with improved agricultural machinery, bread was bound to cheapen, Bill or no Bill. If illustration be wanted of this, we need only reflect that it *still* pays to grow wheat in England (although, of course, upon a steadily decreasing scale), even with the mere cost of freight in favour of the home-grower. The cheapening of bread cannot be fairly attributed wholly to the Corn Laws. As well might the Conservative-Protectionist squire in 1846 point out that wheat had been cheapening, under Protection, since 1812, when it stood at 126 shillings and sixpence a quarter, whereas in 1845 it had fallen to 50s. 10d. a quarter. To this the Cobdenites retorted that it had not cheapened as fast as it ought to have done. Well, that is precisely my contention now: that, although wheat has cheapened since 1846, it has not done so nearly as fast as it should have done; that, after 44 years of Free Trade, it should now be very much lower in price than it is; and, furthermore, that the cause of this slowness has been in abandoning wheat-production to a highly Protective community. Consider how small is, after all, the average difference shown by our tables. Had the same British capital, the same British purchasing-custom, and the same British emigration poured into British territory, wheat would now be far lower in price than it is, because, in no British community has Protection, even when smarting under neglect, been so rigid as in the United States; and, as will later on be shown, the natural tendency of a Colony with settled, thriving industries, is not towards Protection, but towards Free Trade. The younger the Colony, and the more vague its industries, the greater the tendency towards Protection. English neglect and the apparent necessity of working out some sort of independent existence are the chief causes of Colonial tariffs. Thus, whereas the older-established mother Colony of Australasia, New South Wales, is Free Trade in policy, every one of her offshoots is Protectionist.

It must, of course, be understood clearly that, in all this, I have no quarrel with Free Trade principles, but solely with the short-sighted application of those principles, which has resulted in jeopardising the entire fabric of British commerce. John Bright's Colonial policy throughout was " Let them go;" and that policy has been the accepted text of modern so-called Liberalism. That policy has been followed in all but actual repudiation. The trade of the Colonies has been sacrificed, their energies fostered only when the London Stock Exchange saw its chance. England has wooed the foreigner, and the foreigner now turns to rend her with M'Kinley tariffs and French exclusion bills. Had she taken the trouble to inform herself as to the cereal capabilities of her own dominions, she would, by this time, be enjoying a cheaper loaf, the United States would be an out-at-elbows, shin-plastered collection of communities without any Trade at all (they have only a £4 8s. average *now*), and the British Empire would be the most powerful Confederacy in the world.

Why did not England do so? Ah! Why did not Hannibal go on to Rome instead of stopping at Capua? Ignorance, my reader; simple, downright ignorance. Up to within a few years ago, even the best informed Englishmen knew practically nothing of Colonial affairs, whilst popular ignorance upon the subject was really amazing. Letters arriving in Australia, with such superscriptions as " Mr. Dash Blank, Adelaide, near Melbourne, New South Wales," were too common even to raise a laugh. Canada also, although so near, was popularly regarded as a sort of frozen wilderness, where people pursued seals upon toboggans, performed all labour upon snow-shoes, and annually enjoyed a six months' eclipse of the sun. As for the Cape, that simply conjured up visions of storms, diamonds, omnivorous ostriches, and happy Hottentots. Only of late years have the wheat raising potentialities of India been discovered. In fact, the resources of the Empire have been a blank page; although, in reality, but one word fairly describes them,—unlimited.

What Colonial land is actually under crop? In Canada, 11,614,000 acres, besides 280,000 acres under orchard culture. In Australia, 20,771,000 acres, together with an unstated orchard area, which must be considerable, seeing that one township alone, Parramatta, turns out eleven million dozens of oranges annually.

And are these Canadian and Australian areas suitable for wheat? Yes, with the exception of some 4,000,000 acres in the northern portion of New South Wales and in Queensland, where wheat is replaced by maize. The average yield per acre? Taking all cereals grown at present, 17 bushels to the acre, making a total yield of 32,385,000 bushels, or 4,048,125 quarters. This is a mere bagatelle compared to the possible output. At present it is impossible for any Colony to compete with the United States owing to the vast established cereal industries of the latter, their proximity to English markets, and their wheat rings, which rig and rule these markets. But, once let it be known that, on and after a certain date, the American [1] cereals (now worth £18,210,496 out of a total of £36,054,410 imported) will be handicapped by a tariff, and vast areas of British territory, now lying idle, will speedily be brought under cultivation. With modern labour-saving machinery, cereals do not need a large population for their production, and (unlike oxen) they do not take long to grow. So extensive and so geographically varied are our possessions, that cereal crops could be garnered in and despatched to English ports well-nigh all the year round; and this wide distribution of production would destroy the opportunities attendant upon the American crops, to

[1] Russia has been, of late years, England's second great source of supply, our cereal imports for 1889-90 standing as follows:

	Value in £
Wheat	8,002,394
Barley	1,709,389
Oats	3,865,488
Other kinds	1,142,489
	£14,719,460

And although the Russian crops for 1891 have proved so poor as to be insufficient for local consumption and to cause wide-spread famine, this can only be regarded as an exceptional national disaster, unlikely to recur except, possibly, at long intervals. Under normal conditions, the proposals made with respect to American cereals would apply equally to Russian.

limit the output or to play any of the thousand and one tricks so well-known to Chicago corners and Mark Law rings. Thus, within a very few years, the British public would know what cheap bread really means, under the competition of a world-wide Empire.

How long would it take for the united efforts of the Empire to supply England with the present quantity, at present prices? The quantity would be forthcoming at two years' notice, at the outside. The price would probably, at first, be slightly in excess of present rates (the tables show that the difference has never been very alarming). But against that, there would be the certainty of a rapidly falling prospective price: and an increase to the revenue from the duty upon American wheat which, tax or no tax, *must* be thrown upon the English market for what it will fetch, or rot upon Dakota wheat fields.

Grain and Sugar. Grain, other than breadstuffs, does not call for much comment, because each and every variety can be profitably produced to any required extent. What says the English farmer to soil (the Canterbury Plains, New Zealand) which, without an ounce of manure, *averages* 80 bushels of oats to the acre; which oats I have myself known to be unsaleable at sixpence per bushel, within sight of Lyttelton harbour? Barley thrives equally well, but is equally unprofitable. Rice we have already a monopoly of in the East. I have seen samples of hops (Tasmanian, New Zealand, and Victorian) which Kent itself could not surpass, but so little are they in demand that Australian brewers actually import them!

Sugar cannot so lightly be passed over. In this industry, the reckless, bull-at-a-gate perversion of intelligent Free Trade, to which we have given the name of Cobdenism, has led England not only to neglect her own possessions, but to permit one of her own best enterprises—the sugar-refining trade—to be practically crushed out of existence. How did this come about? Very simply. Continental nations invented a sort of double-barrel Protection for sugar by paying bounties upon exports of the refined article. Against this monstrous handicap even England protested—to the extent of appointing Bounties' Commissions and proposing Bounties' Conferences. But it is useless opposing words to brickbats. She did nothing more; and her refining industry perished. There was no second economic reason why it should so have perished. Foreigners have no special knowledge of, or skill in, refining which should entitle them, even upon Free Trade principles, to monopoly in the industry. They were simply bribed at both ends, by Protective tariffs and by bounties, to an extent which closed the English factories. And here are the results.

In 1889, England imported refined sugar from the following countries to the amounts stated.

Germany - - - -	£8,771,220
France - - - -	2,855,268
Holland - - - -	1,692,678
Belgium - - - -	1,077,180
	£14,396,346

In the same year, England exported £609,115 worth of the same commodity; and, most probably, even this paltry quantity was not of English manufacture.

Now, nine-tenths of the known sugar-cane areas are British possessions, of which I need only mention the West Indies, Mauritius, Queensland, and New South Wales, north of the Clarence River. The Dutch have Java, and make full use of it. But where do the other foreigners get their raw sugar from? Some they grow, from beet-root; the rest they import from British possessions, refine, and sell in English markets. Beet-root sugar is said to be of finer quality than cane sugar, and foreigners are specially skilled in beet culture. Perhaps it is; perhaps they are. But if beet be essential for the finer qualities, why not grow it in the Colonies, under far more favourable conditions of soil and climate than exist in Europe? For the commoner sugars, at all events, cane is, and always will be, the staple. And why, in the name of common sense, not place English refiners upon equal terms (at least) with their foreign rivals, and revive this important but extinct industry?

Before we quit this monstrous "bounties" question, we may, parenthetically, note the almost equally unfair system pursued by certain foreign Governments with a view to undermining British shipping interests. Within the past few years, France and Germany, becoming alive to the growing importance of the Australian trade, have heavily subsidised the Messageries Maritimes and the Nord-Deutscher Lloyd Companies respectively, to run fleets of powerful steamships in opposition to the English companies. But for the subsidies, such competition would be impossible; but, with the assistance of the bribe thus given, the foreign companies contrive to keep down English profits to a most unjust extent. The object avowedly is to encourage French and German shipping industries. The real object is to encourage, by low freights, the exportation of Colonial raw material to France and Germany in order that (as with sugar) it may there be manufactured for the English market. Thus, too, the exportation of Colonial wines is growing with great rapidity. It nearly all comes to

England, but it travels *via* France and Germany, to be flavoured up into claret, and hock, and champagne.

How, it may be asked, can the British Government prevent foreign Governments from granting bounties and subsidies, if they see fit to do so? It cannot; it is not suggested that it could. But what is contended is that, under Commercial Union tariffs, foreign refineries and foreign steamers would find their occupation gone, so far, at least, as crippling British industries is concerned. And that is the only point that in any way concerns us.

Fruits and Vegetables. The amount expended upon these is, relatively, not very large, but still quite large enough to merit attention. The vegetables must be grown at home or (with the exception of dried vegetables and, perhaps, potatoes) imported duty free from the Continent. To this no Colony would object in the case of foods, which, from their perishable nature, cannot be Colonial grown. But fruits they can supply, and will insist upon supplying, under a tariff. With careful packing all the ordinary fruits can be imported, from different places, so as to be as plentiful here in spring as in autumn. One of the very best and wholesomest fruits, which seems now to be gaining in public favour, the banana, needs no packing at all. Bunches of luscious "lady's fingers," cut green in Queensland or Fiji, and hung up anywhere on board ship, arrive in London in a ripe condition. There is not the smallest danger of the fruit supply running short. But there will be full scope for English fruit-growers, especially of the choicer and more perishable varieties, to embark extensively in this industry.

Such, then, is a brief analysis of England's food supply, how, and whence, it could be maintained. Our considerations appear to establish three facts of the very utmost economic importance, which may be thus shortly summarised: (1) The British possessions have, even now, resources sufficiently great to supply England's necessities in many important branches, and could do so, at a profit, if favoured by a tariff. (2) With sufficiently long notice to prepare, they could make good such deficiencies as at present exist. And, of course, the longer the notice, the more complete would be the supplies. (3) Supplies, so procured, would not necessarily, or even probably, be notably higher in price than rates now current; and they would, owing to wide and keen competition, tend to fall very much faster than they do now.

IX. *Exchange considerations.*

We must now resume the Trade profit and loss

account, which was postponed at the end of Section IV. for later discussion.

It is clear that, if England transfers her food custom from the outside nations to her own possessions with, perhaps, a share to States in Alliance, these must purchase commodities from her to the value of their increased Trade, which, for food alone, would, as we have seen, amount to £94,013,177. Or, in other words, her proposed new customers would have to increase their export-import trade to the extent of £188,026,354 to make a deal possible in the matter of food. That they could supply the food has been shown at some length; that is, the export part of the business offers no further obstacle. But could they increase their imports correspondingly? In answering this question, it is proposed to disregard possible nations in Alliance, for the moment, altogether; and, furthermore, to merge the food-payment Colonial imports in the wider subject of Colonial importing power generally.

The populations of the nine outside nations enumerated in Section III. amount to 270,000,000 and their Trade with Great Britain to £402,454,057. If, thereto, we add Austria-Hungary (which does a paltry British Trade of £3,678,834, with a population of 42,000,000) we obtain a total of 312,000,000 persons and a Trade of £406,132,891, being an average of

£1 5s. per head. Supposing that Great Britain loses this enormous number of customers of European race, with what is she to replace them? Excluding the population of the United Kingdom, the British Empire contains 292,000,000 of persons, of whom 280,000,000 are Asiatics or coloured. These 292,000,000 do a Trade of £432,000,000, equivalent to £1 9s. 6d. per head, of which 13 shillings is with Great Britain. Taken all round, therefore, each foreigner of European race is, commercially, worth nearly two Dependency subjects. True; and were the average a consistent one amongst all Dependencies, the outlook would be black enough. But it is not. India, and India alone, is responsible for the smallness of the quotient. With 273,000,000 of people she only does a total foreign Trade of £172,000,000, not quite seven shillings per head. Other Eastern dusky folk under our flag number 4,200,000 and have a Trade of £54,000,000, giving a respectable average of £13, whilst the 11,000,000 of Colonials do a total Trade of £191,000,000, equal to £17 6s. per head. And, once more, this average is kept down by the lamentable commercial backwardness of Canada and South Africa, which average respectively £8 5s. and £8 5s. 6d. per head, as compared with the Australasian average of £29 9s. 6d., wherein New South Wales leads with the brilliant return of £41 3s., and

The Trade Economy of Federation. 145

Tasmania "whips in" with £22 4s. Finally, we may note that the Straits Settlements stand far ahead of all, and, as there are but 3,483 Europeans in a population of 568,000, it is evident that skin colour is no bar to Trade. There are absolutely no custom dues whatever in Singapore; ideal Free Trade exists, with a Trade result of £102 per head of population! Of course, it is chiefly a receiving-forwarding Trade; but very handsome commissions must stick to the fingers of the Singapore people for all that.

From these facts and figures it becomes plain that the future trade of Great Britain and of the whole Commercial Union must chiefly depend upon the advances made by backward India and by the backward Colonies. And here not only are the probabilities overwhelmingly strong in favour of such progress under the encouraging stimulus of a Commercial Union, but latest reports are most hopeful. Here is an extract from a review (published in the "Asiatic Quarterly" for January, 1891) of Mr. J. E. O'Connor's Report upon Indian Trade for 1890. " Trade shows a steady increase, exceeding by $5\frac{1}{2}$ per cent. that of 1889. . . There is a growing demand for European luxuries amongst the lower classes of even out-of-the-way districts . . . Exports, which reached the huge total of 105 crores of rupees, increased nearly seven per cent.; and a new industry has got

K

a start, which bids fair to compete with America and Australia, and that is the manufacture of flour, which has been established chiefly in Bombay. Altogether, the report is very satisfactory . . ."[1] In this connection, we may pause to note the reason why the averages, not alone of England's Indian, but even of her European and American, customers are so low. They have all extremely small total foreign Trade averages (as will be seen by reference to appendix note on Foreign Trade), which (in the case of Europe and America) their policy tends, in its very nature, to crush. They rely upon internal local commerce. Nothing in the whole range of Trade Economy is so indisputably proved as that "the freer the trade, the greater the trade." Indian Trade policy is free enough, the only imports taxed, besides liquors, being opium, petroleum, and salt. Hence, as the condition of her people gradually improves, and as their growing taste for foreign commodities increases, there is nothing whatever to impede their commercial progress. She cannot be expected, as a result of the Commercial Union, to spring at a bound to the level of her Asiatic sister-dependencies, with their £13 per

---

[1] The reader is earnestly urged to keep himself periodically informed as to Trade returns. As time wears on he will, it is confidently asserted, find the moderate forecasts in this work being gradually verified.

head. But it is impossible to doubt that, within a few years, her Trade would reach a £1 average. What her commerce *must* eventually become it almost dazzles the imagination to contemplate.

It is not easy to understand why Canada and the Cape Colonies are, commercially, so far behind their Australian sisters; nor has a brief residence both in the Dominion and in South Africa afforded me personally much light on the subject. It is, naturally, extremely important to thoroughly appreciate the causes, whatever they may be, with a view to their speedy removal. Protection cannot be the sole explanation, because the Australasian Colonies are, with one exception, Protectionist also, and the Cape is very lightly Protected. Distance from European markets is enormously in their favour. Both are rich in natural resources. Wherein lies the explanation? It is vain to consult Canadian and South African authorities, since one finds therein little else save references to "national prosperity" and "commercial progress." *En voici la preuve.*

	Area in sq.-in.	Population.	Revenue. £	Trade. £
Australia	3,171,978	4,200,000	25,500,000	122,000,000
Cape Colonies	295,000	2,900,000	4,500,000	24,000,000
Canada	3,470,257	5,000,000	7,550,000	43,000,000

The reader will at once see that both the Cape and

Canada are, alike in Revenue and Trade, in reality, miserably deficient. (In nearly all British communities Revenue depends upon Trade; and the curious fact holds, generally, good that the former is one-fifth or one-sixth of the latter.) Perhaps it is, broadly, true to say that Canada has been commercially overshadowed and stunted by her proximity to the United States; and that the Cape has not yet recovered from the deadly blow inflicted upon her by the Suez Canal. If this view be the correct one, then emphatically both are more deserving of pity than of blame. In the case of Canada, what very brilliant results could come of intimate commercial relations with a country which has itself but a beggarly Trade average of £4 8s., especially when that country took the cream of the English Trade? Let it, therefore, be placed to Canada's credit that, in spite of neglect, and treaties, and overshadowing, she can show double the American Trade average. And let her, moreover, despite immediate commercial loss and confusion, welcome the M'Kinley tariff as a blessing in disguise, since it compels her to embark in newer and more profitable channels, and is the strongest lever ever forged to bring about a Britannic Commercial Union. Her Trade, henceforth, must increase, as surely as a wheel, when the brake is removed, will run down an incline.

So, too, with the Cape, which has by this time realised that her destiny is something greater than to be a mere calling place for eastward-bound ships. What say statistics? Do they indicate any increase of late years in Canadian and South African Trade? Fortunately, an eminent authority, Sir Rawson Rawson, has prepared tables which fully answer these questions as regards the whole Empire, and more especially so far as England's Trade is concerned.

Table showing Increase of British Trade.

Trade of United Kingdom with—	Amount.		Percentage proportion.		Percentage Increase in 1889 compared with average of 1884-8.
	Average of 1884-8. £Millions.	1889. £Millions.	Average of 1884-8.	1889.	
British India and Straits Settlements	71·5	76·4	10·9	10·3	6·8
British North America	19·3	21·6	3·0	3·0	11·7
Australasia	50·5	52·2	7·7	7·0	3·5
South Africa (Cape of Good Hope and Natal)	10·0	15·9	1·5	2·1	58·6
All other Colonies ..	16·6	17·9	2·5	2·4	7·4
Total	167·9	184·0	25·6	24·8	9·5

These results appear to set the question as to the expansion of Colonial Trade definitely at rest. The strides made by the Cape are truly astounding; a fifty-eight per cent. increase effected, as it were, at a bound! Such progress is quite unparalleled, and very plainly proves the commercial vitality of the

Colony. Canada, with an increase of nearly 12 per cent., speaks as to her prospects in no uncertain tones. All the rest show up well, with the exception of Australasia; and the cause of her small increase must assuredly lie in the fact that her Trade has for the past ten years, nay, throughout, been already phenomenally great for so small a population. It is especially cheering to observe that these are all increases in Trade with Great Britain; of course, the justification and very heart's blood of a Britannic Commercial Union. How is it possible to doubt, in the face of such recent evidence, and hampered as Colonial Trade still is, that under a Union each of the Colonies would speedily attain to an average at least equal to that of the Australian group, or that the average of the latter would rapidly soar towards three figures? And surely if ever solid premisses justified an impending conclusion, then the following forecast is warranted by existing facts.

British Trade at time of establishment of the Britannic Commercial Union, i.e. Present Trade with 5 per cent. added for increase between now and then.

Great Britain's Total Foreign and Colonial Trade	£779,481,292
Total Trade of Colonies and Dependencies	453,198,707
	£1,232,686,999

The Trade Economy of Federation. 151

British Trade twelve months after Commercial Union.

India and Straits Settlements	£560,000,000
North American Colonies	98,000,000
Australasian Colonies	206,000,000
South African Colonies	64,000,000
All others	40,000,000
	£968,000,000
States in Alliance	224,000,000
	£1192,000,000
United Kingdom[1]	£714,000,000
Total British Trade	{ 968,000,000 { 714,000,000
	£1,682,000,000

The attention of the reader is drawn to the facts that not only are the above totals based upon very carefully-considered premisses, but a lavish margin remains for any possible shortcomings: the estimated total British Trade, consequent upon the Union, is five hundred and eight millions larger than it is at present, and four hundred and fifty millions larger than it could reasonably be expected to be upon existing lines, two years hence—were there no such disturbing influences ahead as increased foreign tariffs and time-expiring treaties. It may be added that it is far more probable that Great Britain's share

[1] Allowing two-thirds of the Colonial and Dependency Trade (at present England's share is three-sevenths); and one-third of the Alliance Trade.

of the total has been understated than that the total itself has been exaggerated.

X. Would the tendency of such a Commercial Union be towards Protection or Free Trade?

Once more, let us proceed cautiously and tentatively. Now, although politics are beyond the scope of the present work, it is impossible to ignore the fact that Commercial Union will inevitably entail some form of political confederation. That is to say, that instead of each section of the Empire basing its Trade policy upon the theory of eventual independent national existence, the aspirations of all will be abundantly satisfied by existing as responsible, legislating units of a world-wide Britannic whole. Healthy rivalry then will be just as there now is between Yorkshire and Middlesex, or between Ontario and Quebec; but alienation of national sentiment there will be none. And, hence, the greatest existing prop to Protection amongst the Colonies will be withdrawn so soon as the word "Colony" is erased from our statute-books. The trading instinct is innate in communities of British race, and chafes at the restraint which national expediency (or what has been held to be national expediency) has placed upon freedom of Trade. Remove the restraint, and race will follow its instincts.

It may be stated, with almost the precision of a mathematical formula, that the closer the bonds of union are drawn between communities of the same race, the greater will be the Trade between them, the disturbing element being the distance separating such communities. Or, mathematically, commerce [between such communities] varies directly as Union and inversely as distance, *i.e.*:

$$\text{Commerce} = \frac{\text{Union}}{\text{Distance}}$$

Hence:

The closer the Union, the greater the Trade.

The greater the Trade, the more general the desire for unrestricted or Free Trade.

As a corollary to this general law, it follows that every effort made towards strengthening the bonds of union, or diminishing distance (which, economically, means more rapid and more extensive means of intercommunication), tends directly towards increasing the volume of commerce. Until Commercial Union becomes an accomplished fact, railroads and steamships must be the principal adjuncts to swelling Board of Trade returns. The beneficial effects of the Canadian Pacific Railway and of the promised fleet of Canadian Liners have yet to make themselves felt.[1]

---

[1] The recent record-time, nineteen days, made between Tokio and London, *via* this very railway, and the fast mail boats in connection therewith, is a brilliant illustration of this position.

After a few years of the Protective encouragement afforded by the Commercial Union to British communities against foreigners, such Colonial industries as were built upon a sound productive basis could gradually dispense with Protection within the Union. This may seem to be at variance with our well-established previous contention that Protection tends to intensify and not to diminish. But it is not. The uncompromising, headstrong, all-producing Protection begotten of national expediency does tend to intensify; it is as insatiable as the daughters of the horse-leech. It is, however, radically different from the discriminating, economically sound Protection, adopted in order to enable young and backward States of a self-contained Empire to give their productive powers a fair test. Let us take an example. In the Illawarra district of New South Wales, at Wollongong and Bulli, there are inexhaustible seams of the finest steam-coal in the world—coal that never "cakes," coal, that stokers say, "it is a treat to handle." Within fifty miles of this coal there are large deposits of iron ore. Naturally, attempts have been made to start iron industries. But such industries require large capital for their inception, and money is dear in the Colony. They require skilled labour, which is scarce and dear also. Still might all these difficulties be surmounted but for foreign competition. It is simply hopeless for the Colonial ironmaster to attempt to undersell Germany and the United States, to say nothing of England and Scotland. He appeals for Protection, but, as the policy of New South Wales is Free Trade, he appeals in vain. The iron rests undisturbed in the Blue Mountains: which are celebrated for their scenery. There are upwards of thirty rich, unworked coal-seams at Wollongong, which town, however, enjoys its chief reputation for its butter. Now, is there any valid economic reason why an industry, so favoured by natural conditions, should not be fostered during its struggling infancy? None whatever. Adam Smith himself would so have fostered it. Or is there any reason why it should require continued Protection after it once took firm root? None. Then, why was not an exception made in its favour? Free Trade permits no such exceptions, as Free Trade is, at present, understood. Yet, in this particular, glaring instance, the New South Wales Government *has* ventured a little way, by accepting a few local contracts for iron manufactures at an increase upon import rates.

Examples might be multiplied; but one suffices to illustrate the distinction between the economically-sound Protection of encouragement and the economically-rotten Protection of exclusion.

In intimate connection with the question as to the duration of Protective tariffs is the subject of labour. The Colonial working-man stands upon a very much higher platform than his brother in the United Kingdom, whom he regards with the utmost pity and not a little contempt. He derives all his information from an ultra-radical press which is never so happy as when it can harp upon the " down-trodden condition of the British labouring classes," or the latest " death from starvation in a London garret." In a country of manhood-suffrage, he is master of the situation, and he has very nearly found it out. He has achieved a signal victory in the Eight Hours Labour Limit Acts; and now he has plunged into a war against capital, in which he has, so far, come off second best. In his secret soul, he does not recognise that capital has any rights whatever. He believes it to be a dishonestly-worked pool, filled by the proceeds of his labour, and out of which he never receives his fair dividend. And so long as his economic education is left in the hands of ignorant demagogues, who fatten upon his credulity, he will continue so to fight and so to believe. Of late years, British working-men have been stimulated into following his example, have striven to make their Trades Unions as far-reaching as his, and have gone on strike with even greater frequency. They are still worse advised than the Colonial; or, perhaps, it is fairer to say that their political power is not sufficiently great to enable them to take his preliminary measures. To fight capital, even after it has been weakened by an Eight Hours Act, is a desperate venture. To attempt to fight it without such an Act is sheer insanity. The market value of all labour is regulated by supply, that is, by competition. Once the minimum daily wage has been reached (the limit, below which labour cannot subsist), further competition narrows itself down to the number of hours of work *per diem*. If this be limited by law to eight hours, capital at once loses a principal source of cheap labour, and all further contest centres round the amount to be paid for eight hours' daily work. This the Colonial had sense enough to grasp; but his British brethren have only faint glimmerings of it, and it is clearly not the policy of Messrs. Mann, Tillett, Burns, & Co., to open their eyes. There is something almost pitiful in the sight of a deputation of working-men waiting upon the Nestor of British politics for his views upon the Eight Hours' question. He had none; it is, politically, too dangerous to express views upon so unbending a science as Social Economy. They were informed that the subject demanded the most patient consideration; which, being interpreted, means, either that an ex-Premier and Chancellor of the Exchequer is avowedly ignorant of the very elements of Economy, or, that he is waiting to see which side of the question the political cat will jump.

The broad fact is that it is well-nigh impossible for a modern politician who is, necessarily, a seeker after place and a holder of candles to the Protean devil of public opinion to be also an Economist, who is a seeker after truth.

The capitalist denies the right of the Legislature to place any time-restriction upon his employment of labour. But this, as we know, is a mere beating the air. There is no such element as abstract right or wrong in Social Economy. Whatever is expedient for the time being is right, whatever is inexpedient is wrong. Trade is obviously expedient. It has been shown that a Commercial Union is expedient. Therefore every measure necessary to establish that Union, upon the most expedient lines, is expedient also. These "most expedient lines" tend, from our point of view, towards an ultimate policy of Free Trade throughout the Union. The only point, therefore, which concerns us is to inquire whether or not an Eight Hours Act would be such a measure.

Protective tariffs in the Colonies will subsist so long as may be necessary to place naturally favoured local industries upon a footing of being able to compete successfully in local markets. The most expensive element in production is labour. So long as British labour remains disproportionately cheap as compared with Colonial labour, the tariffs must remain. So soon as the price of British labour, superadded to the cost of freight, balances the cost of Colonial labour, there is no further necessity for tariffs. If workmen in the Colonies are both better paid and work fewer hours than in Great Britain, how can equilibrium ever be restored? It is impossible to regulate wages by Act of Parliament. But it is quite possible to regulate hours of work. Let, therefore, the Legislature do what it can, and remove half the difficulty of equalising the labour markets. The wages part will right itself in time by emigration from overcrowded to undermanned centres of industry. Meanwhile capitalists would find more profitable employment in seeking to disseminate amongst their workmen a more intelligent appreciation of the meaning of distribution, than in goading these very men to insurrection, and in offending the ears of Economists by continued assertion of "rights" which are seen only by the light of nature, and exist chiefly in their own imaginations. They have their rights; but employment of labour for twelve or fifteen hours a-day is not one of them.

The reader will readily perceive how important an influence this labour question will hereafter play in shaping future Colonial Trade policy; and that whatsoever tends to bring the labour markets throughout the Empire to, at least approximately, equal conditions of work-time and means of subsistence, tends also towards uniformity in tariffs, towards gradual abolition of the latter as unnecessary, and, hence, towards intercivil Free Trade. It is, therefore, distinctly expedient that the political cat should forthwith jump for eight hours; and, if working-men be wise, they will, instead of damaging themselves and their cause by a succession of temper-begotten strikes, devote all their energies towards securing an Eight Hours Labour Act. It lies within their power to do this by constitutional methods, which alone command the approval and support of the nation at large.

We have said that wage equilibrium must be left to work itself out by time and increased migration facilities. We may go farther and point out that even now the difference is not so overwhelmingly upon the side of the Colonial as is here popularly supposed. Let us seize the opportunity to enliven our somewhat heavy economic enquiries by a few pen-and-ink sketches in illustration of this misconception.

Sheep-farming, as everybody knows, is a staple Australian industry, and of course furnishes employment to a great many men at shearing-time. The days of that hermit of the plains, the shepherd, have been pretty well numbered by the modern system of wire-fencing. Still any one with a taste for a secluded life may obtain a job in what is grimly termed the "never, never" back country. But what seclusion! A visit at intervals of three weeks or a month from a boundary-rider bringing provisions of flour, sugar, tea, and tobacco, with, perhaps, a mutilated newspaper three months old. Salt meat in plenty, and fresh mutton if he cares to kill and skin a sheep. Wages, one pound a week, which he usually draws annually. Not in cash; no cash is ever seen upon a station; but in the form of a cheque. Then comes off the event of the year, the long-looked-forward-to "spree." The cheque is handed over to the proprietor of the nearest "shanty" (bush public-house), and all-comers are bidden to assist in "knocking it down." "Blue ruin" (manufactured from new rum, tobacco, and *bluestone*) does the rest. A fit of *delirium tremens*, cured (or killed) by a few days' incarceration in an out-house, a farewell "nip with the boss," supplemented by a bottle of ruin to put in his swag, and our shepherd returns to his sheep for another year's solitude.

Shearers, if skilled hands, earn large wages. But the work is terribly severe, with no protection from a scorching sun except a galvanised iron roof. Wages used to be ten shillings per score of sheep, and, as a good shearer can get through fourscore in a day, the end of the season found him with a very comfortable sum in hand. But the distances to be traversed from station to station are often very great; and, since the introduction of the Wolseley shearing-machine, work has become less plentiful and worse paid. Moreover, at the best of times, shearing was only a temporary employment.

Stockmen earn about £30 a year, with rations and a sleeping bunk. But to be a stockman, one must be able to sit buck-jumping horses for twelve hours a day under a hot sun, to cut out a wild bullock with a stock whip, of which the last is five yards long, and to do odd jobs of fencing and rough carpentering which need some knowledge of tools. The life is healthy enough and seems to have a fascination for those engaged in it. The food is abundant, more remarkable, indeed, for abundance than variety: "damper" (dough baked in ashes), beef, tea, and sugar, which may be supplemented by private purchases of various tinned luxuries. Such articles as vegetables, eggs, butter, etc., are seldom even heard of.

"Wanted for a station, married couple. Man to do farm work. Wife to cook, wash, and be generally useful. Wages, £40." Such is an every-day advertisement; and, of course, speaks for itself.

"Wanted a governess to teach and take entire charge of seven children. Must have thorough knowledge of music and French. German and elementary Latin desirable. Salary, £18 a year." This is equally common, and is incidentally set down by way of caution to fair members of the writer's own profession.

Miners are the best paid of all. Gold miners, alike in Ballarat (Victoria) and in Charters Towers (Queensland), average from ten to eleven shillings per day of eight hours. Coal miners earn more, especially skilled men paid by results. Some, employed in the Bulli-Wollongong district, figure upon the fortnightly pay-sheets for as much as £12 and even £14. Others, less skilled, or less industrious, receive but £7 to £8. But the industry has never been a very steady one. Employment is not always to be had, and subscriptions to the "Strike Fund" are heavy. Again, the conditions of life are, to the last degree, monotonous. No places of amusement to go to, except an occasional circus or travelling theatrical show; a thirst-begetting climate, during a great portion of the year, which causes the inevitable hotels to be crowded places of resort; the evil national custom of "shouting" (standing treat) for a crowd, no matter how numerous. All these circumstances conspire to discount the value of the wages earned. It is a common saying of new arrivals that "one pound in the old country is better than two out here;" and, broadly, the remark is accurate enough.

In the large cities, life is very much the same as in English centres. Wages are, all round, a little higher, and the hours, of course, are far easier. The common food necessaries are cheaper; house rent and clothing dearer. Upon the whole, the Colonial artisan has probably two shillings over, upon Saturday night, to every one his British kinsman can call his own. But in all the luxuries and distractions of life, the Englishman has an enormous advantage. The "wonderful penny" is rarely used in Australia; its place is taken by the threepenny piece. "Halves of four ale" and "twos of rum hot" are unknown terms. Threepence is the lowest tender in any Colonial bar, whilst higher toned places draw the line at sixpence. Tobacco is dearer, and so are all places of amusement, which latter are, furthermore, naturally behind the English standard, both in variety and quality. These may, to some, appear trivial points, but to the British workman they represent the very salt of existence. Let him be careful, therefore, not to confound the number with the purchasing power of the shillings earned as wages. Let him emigrate by all means, if he finds things going badly with him at home; but let him not start with exaggerated expectations of what awaits him at the other side of the world. Lastly, it cannot be too well or too widely known that the immigrant most wanted and most desired is the agriculturalist; if married, so much the better. Favoured by liberal Land Acts, he can select a homestead in any one of the Colonies, where, with good soil beneath his feet, and a blue sky overhead, it is entirely his own fault if he does not prosper. And if the Commercial Union should show signs of becoming an accomplished fact, Colonists like him will more than ever be needed to bring now idle soil into profitable production.

XI. Financial effects of a Commercial Union.

We have only to reflect upon the enormous amount of British capital invested in the thousands of channels known to the London money market to appreciate at once the full importance of this section in our inquiry. It is unnecessary that we should seek to bring the amount down to exact, or even approximate, figures. It is more to our present purpose to ask, what does this capital represent? How is it chiefly, at present, invested? How would such existing investments be affected by what would be, practically, a revolution in our present commercial policy?

Well, of course, all capital is a saving up of the results of past production. It may be hoarded; in which case it is simply dormant or temporarily unproductive; or it may be utilised; in which case it is active or reproductive. Very few persons actually hoard. A very large number of persons regard security as of infinitely more importance than profit. A smaller number are bolder and endeavour to combine good profit with good security. Whilst a smaller number still are rash, and plunge headlong into mere speculations, which must mean either considerable gain or considerable, if not total, loss. British investments may be broadly classified under two headings: Government securities, British and foreign; industrial enterprises at home and abroad. In both classes of investments, the expected rate of profit or interest is based upon the real or supposed stability of the securities selected. Thus, amongst Government stocks, an investor with, say, £100 might, upon, say, the 14th January, 1891, have chosen, for example, amongst the following :

	Price	Rate of Interest Yielded.
		£ s. d.
British 2½ per cents.	93½	2 13 5
Canadian 3 „	93	3 4 6
New South Wales 3½ per cents.	102¼	3 8 5
New Zealand 4 per cents.	106	3 15 6
French 3 „	97¼	3 3 8
Chilian 4½ „	93	4 16 9
Argentina 5 „	75	6 13 4
Uruguay 6 „	56	10 14 3

These rates exactly reflected the supposed stability and solvency of the communities quoted, and, furthermore, indicated the credit or borrowing-power of these communities. And hence it is of the very utmost importance that national credit should stand as high as possible. Of course, this national credit is a very ticklish thing, and is, in the case of a great many communities, liable to extraordinary fluctuations, and often enough upon little or no grounds. Thus to a person familiar with the two Republics, it is quite unintelligible why the credit of Argentina should stand so much higher than that of its smaller but comparatively far richer neighbour, Uruguay. It may seem strange also that the credit of Canada, which, as we have seen, is commercially and financially far behind New South Wales, should yet be better than that of the sister Colony. But there is a reason for this. The British Government has upon several occasions guaranteed Canadian loans (a proceeding which other Colonies view rather jealously), and this has imparted a value to Canadian credit generally, which it would, otherwise, certainly not enjoy. Moreover, the fact that the Canadian provinces are federated as a Dominion is viewed by investors as an element of strength. Now, clearly, if Federation upon so small a scale be thus favourably regarded, in conjunction with the support of Great Britain, Federation of the Empire, upon the far wider lines foreshadowed by a Commercial Union, would very materially strengthen the credit of all British communities, including that of Great Britain herself. The security offered to investors would be as absolutely safe as can possibly be imagined; and the borrowing powers of the various sections of the Empire would be very materially improved. It is true that the credit of what we have termed outside nations would be impaired by loss of their British Trade, and that holders of foreign securities would thereby suffer, but not to any disastrous extent, the foreign Trade of these nations being, as we know, but a small item in their national polity. Whilst, upon the other hand, the credit of the numerous smaller nations which would, almost to a certainty, join in Commercial Alliance, would greatly improve by being in touch with our Commercial Union; and it is especially these smaller nations, which have absorbed an enormous amount of British capital both in loans and in industrial enterprises, which need strengthening in the interests of their British creditors. The reader will recollect how the Argentina crisis of 1890 brought about the fall of the great financial house of Baring Brothers, and how very barely averted was a wholesale crash in London in consequence. Besides, such British investors as have a fancy for European Government stocks must be perfectly well aware that their securities are absolutely at the mercy of a great war, which may burst forth at any moment. Those who believe in Russian and French bonds, in the teeth of the Triple Alliance, and with the results of the coming struggle a sealed book to human foresight, cannot, with any decency, cry out against the comparatively trivial effects of a Britannic Commercial Union upon their foreign interests. It is open to them to sell out these interests and re-invest in better paying and really far safer Colonial securities.

The same argument applies, with equal force, to industrial enterprises. It is quite true that a very large amount of British capital is invested, for example, in the United States, which would be injuriously affected by the proposed Union. It must, therefore, be for the owners of this capital to use their own judgment as to the likelihood of the Union becoming a fact, and either withdraw their capital from the United States, or leave it there, according to their opinions. It is not proposed to spring the Union as a surprise upon the world. It must, under the most favourable circumstances, take a considerable time to bring about—certainly quite long enough to enable them to shift their eggs from foreign to British baskets. They are not asked to do so from merely patriotic motives which, of course, find no place in hard, economic argument. They are only invited to consider whether it will pay them best to encourage British or foreign enterprises, should the proposals outlined in this work show signs of assuming definite shape.

XII. Foreign nations and the Britannic Commercial Union.

It may be assumed, as a foregone conclusion, that many persons will oppose the Union as a distinct secession from what has been somewhat vaguely termed the "comity of nations." So it most unquestionably would be. But if we inquire what "comity of nations" actually means, and into the grounds of our proposed secession therefrom, the objection will be found to have in it nothing of force or weight. Politically, the "comity of nations" is an elegant way of saying: "Plunder your neighbours if you can, and be very careful lest they plunder you." Commercially it means: "Buy as little as possible from foreigners; sell them all you possibly can." Thus Prussia has, during the recollection of men still middle-aged, raised herself, by a series of successful wars and annexations of adjoining territories, from a second-rate position to the chief place in a powerful Germanic Confederation. Thus, too, Russia has extended, and threatens still further to extend, her dominions at the expense of Turkey; whilst the independent existence of half-a-dozen small kingdoms may, at any moment, be extinguished by a fresh war.

So far as Europe is concerned, Great Britain has no interest in this international game of beggar-my-neighbour, other than to add her weight towards the maintenance of a balance of power amongst the hostile communities, and to keep open the Trade route to the east. She neither covets additional territory in Europe, nor has she much reason to fear a successful attack upon her own shores. Her chief interests are bound up in her outlying dominions, and in her Trade with these. Her commercial policy is also at complete variance with that of other nations. In short, she is only geographically an European power at all. When, in addition to all this, we reflect that other nations do their very utmost, by stringent Protective tariffs, to paralyse international commercial relations, it becomes evident that, in forming a Union of her own peoples, she would merely be building up and strengthening markets to replace those which foreigners have closed to her. Their persistent policy has left her no alternative.

England is the hub upon which revolves such Trade as a heavily-protected world has still left possible. The adoption by England of a new position, as the centre of a Britannic Commercial Union, must necessarily tend to confine Trade, in the widest meaning of the word, within the boundaries of the British Empire, and of the States in Alliance. And although foreign nations have succeeded in reducing their international Trade relations to very low averages per head of population, it may safely be predicted that curtailment of even this small amount will be seriously felt in foreign commercial centres. Without the enterprise, the energy, and the example of English business-houses to stimulate it, European commerce will gradually be exterminated by Protection. Evil days, too, will be in store for New York, and Boston, and Chicago. But these losses will be no fault or doing of ours. We have our own salvation to work out. Let other nations work out theirs.

The first symptom experienced by the outside nations will be a great falling-off in receipts from customs, consequent upon diminished imports. This deficiency will have to be met by a corresponding increase in direct taxation; and it will severely tax the ingenuity of ministers of finance to find out how the screw may be applied with a minimum of popular discontent.

Considerable numbers of operatives will be thrown out of employment, consequent upon diminished exports. And of these, it is probable that a large proportion, especially of the more skilled artisans, will emigrate to British Colonies, since the United States will be productively as much checked as Europe. This apparently inevitable loss of population will make the double burthen of meeting the revenue and of filling the regiments all the harder upon those who remain; and popular discontent will be redoubled. It will soon become apparent that communities within our Union will be gaining exactly in proportion as foreign nations will be losing; and outcries abroad will be redoubled. Foreign powers will see the very cream of their populations abandoning stagnation and conscription for progress and freedom. They will see their revenues steadily decreasing, and their recruiting-grounds as steadily becoming exhausted. They will find the torrent of popular clamour yearly becoming harder to dam up and restrain within bounds. And they will see in the future nothing but continued aggravation of these evils.

God forbid that any of these reflections should be imputed to any base gloating by anticipation over coming foreign troubles. They are set down in no malice, but in order to lead up to what it would seem must be the final outcome.

The strain of maintaining millions of unproductive troops is, even now, borne with the utmost difficulty, and, solely, from a general conviction that they are absolutely necessary as a safeguard to national existence. Philanthropists, appalled at the preparations made for slaughter upon a scale hitherto unprecedented in the world's history, talk desperately about national disarmament. Disarmament! while yet the German holds Alsace, and the Turk Constantinople? Vain hope! So far as human foresight can anticipate coming events, the European crash is merely a question of time, of how long it may be possible for the existing strain upon national resources to be endured. So soon as any one of the great powers finds itself unable to bear the prolonged suspense of armed preparation, it must, in self-defence, precipitate matters; nor are signs wanting that, by at least two of them, this stage has nearly been reached. Moreover, the balance of power is so evenly adjusted that no nation, or probable coalition of nations, can hope for an easy victory. The Triple Alliance may, or may not, prove staunch; may, or may not, prove triumphant. It is just as easy to suppose that it may fall to pieces, or be crushed by a Franco-Russian combination. But whichever way the impending struggle may end, it will inevitably leave victors and vanquished alike utterly exhausted. That will be the moment for a peace-loving, disinterested power to interpose with benefit to mankind; but in order to do so effectually, that power must itself be strong enough to make its voice respected. Great Britain, as she stands, is certainly not such a power; it is even doubtful whether, upon her present lines of policy, she could escape being herself dragged into the war, and it is a very open question as to how much of her Empire would remain under her flag at the finish. But Great Britain, as the leading State of a world-wide Confederation, would be such a power. And inasmuch as the establishment of a Commercial Union is, so far as may be judged from past and current events, an essential preliminary to such a Confederation, it follows that the Union, in addition to offering salvation to British Trade, offers also the very best prospects for the future of the world's peace. The expediency of, indeed the necessity for, Protection in the case of nations compelled to resort to vast armaments has already been indicated in some detail. And if it can be made possible for these armaments to be dispensed with, the strongest barrier against foreign Free Trade will be removed. Then, and not till then, will the "comity of nations" become a reality, and have an intelligible, well-defined significance in British ears.

XIII. Steps towards a Britannic Commercial Union.

Evidently the first thing necessary is to thoroughly arouse public opinion throughout the Empire as to the necessity for such a Union. Once the importance of the question becomes generally recognised, measures will soon follow. Colonial Chambers of

Commerce will naturally look to London for a lead, and London is not likely to be backward in setting it. Nothing so strongly furthers a genuine, healthy movement of this sort, as the bringing together of representative commercial men and politicians from all parts of the Empire. These men give expression to the views, desires, and requirements of the communities which they represent; and it becomes possible to decide upon bases as nearly as possible in accordance with the wishes of all. But not less is it essential that these communities should themselves rightly appreciate their own best interests, in order that their delegates may set out with a clearly defined mission. A few such Trade Congresses would result in an agreement upon, at least, the broad outlines of a Commercial Code, which could be subsequently perfected at leisure.

Nor is it to be supposed that the expediency of holding such Trade Congresses has been overlooked by the distinguished men who have made the future welfare of our Empire their especial study. Indeed, as will be seen from a brief epitome of the work already done, the idea of commercial reciprocity has already taken fairly strong root, and needs but a more pronounced support from the various sections of the British race to grow into accomplished fact.

Upon the 12th of February (1891), the Earl of

Dunraven moved the following resolution in the House of Lords:

"That, in the opinion of this House, it is desirable that the Colonial Governments be invited to send representatives to a Conference, to be held in London, to consider the advancement of Trade within Her Majesty's dominions, and the formation of a fund for certain purposes of Imperial defence."

Lord Salisbury, in reply, stated that Her Majesty's Government thought that "for the present the summoning of a Conference was not expedient." And the Premier based his objections upon the following considerations: (*a*) The Colonies would need to debate the entire question thoroughly before they could entrust their delegates with any definite proposals; (*b*) the state of opinion in Great Britain made it impossible "for any statesman, whatever his opinion may be, to propose the establishment of retaliatory duties"; (*c*) the articles primarily affected would be grain, wool, and meat; and (asked his lordship) "What chance have you of inducing the people of this country to accept legislation which would make these essential articles of consumption susceptible of such tariffs?" But he added: "Whenever such a modification of opinion takes place, so that this idea of discrimination of duties in favour of the Colonies shall be a fiscal possibility, I, at all events, shall not oppose the wish of my noble friend to have the matter thoroughly discussed between ourselves and the Colonies." And, in the end, Lord Dunraven withdrew his motion.

Now, the grain, wool, and meat difficulties have been discussed at some length in this work, and do not, upon examination, appear to be so insuperable as Lord Salisbury appears to believe. But his lordship is clearly right in insisting that public opinion must first be educated before reciprocal tariff legislation can even be hinted at by an English statesman— "whatever his opinion may be."

In the month of April, the inauguration of the United Empire Trade League marked a long step forward toward the goal of Britannic Commercial Union, and the first manifesto issued by Colonel Howard Vincent, C.B., M.P., honorary secretary to the League, admirably epitomises the great question. Writes the gallant Colonel in conclusion:

"To elicit the voice of the nation—of the Empire, of the British race—on this great question; to develop the world-wide internal commerce, on mutually advantageous terms, of the British Empire, is the object of the United Empire Trade League. It seeks your support—it hopes for your active sympathy and co-operation in whatever sphere you are, in whatever portion of the realm of Britain and Greater Britain you may be located."

On June 19th, a strong deputation of the United Empire Trade League, including fifteen members of Parliament, had an interview with Lord Salisbury. The objects of the League were thus formulated :

(1) To free the Mother Country and the Empire from the treaty engagements with Foreign Powers which prevented the Colonies from giving any preference to British Trade; and (2) to summon an Imperial Conference to consider the most practicable plan of bringing the various portions of the Empire into closer commercial union.

After listening to the able arguments advanced in support of these objects, Lord Salisbury replied at some length and very much to the same effect as he had replied to Lord Dunraven's resolution. His lordship's concluding remarks ran as follows :

"The difficulties have been often stated, but I will just refer to them again. If you give a preferential treatment—that is, a better price—to your Colonies, it must be a better price than that which, with unrestricted competition, is obtaining now. A better price to the producer means a more disagreeable price to the consumer; and what we have to know before we can formulate any propositions, or before we can invite our Colonies to any kind of federation, is how far the people of this country would be disposed to support a policy of which, I imagine, the most prominent features are preferential taxes on corn, preferential taxes on meat, and preferential taxes on wool. Some people may say you can have those preferential taxes without any increase of price to the consumer. Here we are going into the recesses of Economical Science, into which I will not ask you to follow me, even if I were competent to take you through them; but I ask you to give to your propositions that sharpness and definiteness in order that these matters may be thrashed out and argued out before the country. You will never get your countrymen to consent to legislation of a vague or indefinite kind, especially on matters which concern their dearest daily interests. If they are to make a sacrifice, or if they are to depart from their previous policy in a manner which you convince them involves no sacrifice, they will, at all events, desire to know it in detail and to be thoroughly convinced of the soundness of the arguments by which you have arrived at the convictions you are urging upon them. I know that the ordinary view of the duties of the Government is to devise for itself the measures that it will bring forward, and to bring them forward and let them take their chance. However true that may be—and I have no doubt it is in a great measure true with respect to the large mass of legislation on secondary questions which they have to propose—it is not true with respect to an organic question which concerns and will control the very existence of our Empire and the very foundations of our Trade. On these matters public opinion must be formed before any Government can act. No Government can impose its own opinion upon the people of this country in these matters. It is the duty of those who feel themselves to be the leaders of such a movement and the apostles of such a doctrine to go forth and fight for it, and when they have convinced the people of this country their battle will be won."

These masterly words once more emphasise the paramount necessity of educating public opinion— even to the extent of leading it "into the recesses of Economical Science." Now these recesses are, after all, not so deeply hidden as to lie beyond the grasp of the most ordinary intelligence, as it is hoped the reader of these pages will concede. Finally, the London Chamber of Commerce has resolved to convene a Congress of Chambers of Commerce of the Empire, to be held in June, 1892.

It cannot be expected that any definite scheme of Commercial Union will then be agreed to by the delegates, because it requires years, not months, to form public opinion upon a question of such magnitude. Under our free British institutions, enjoyed equally by the British throughout our vast Empire, legislation cannot advance one inch in advance of public opinion. We are legislatively a slow-moving race; nor does our history belie the wisdom of our forefathers' extreme deliberation in the past. But it must be borne in mind that events, in the political and commercial world, shape themselves nowadays with far greater rapidity than formerly, and that our opinions must be formed so as to keep pace with nineteenth century progress. We hold a vast heritage in trust for our posterity, but we hold it with a grasp which must be tightened, or, assuredly, bit by bit, it will slip away. And as a matter not merely of probability, but of self-evident certainty, what so sure of tightening that grasp as Commercial Union amongst essentially commercial communities?

THE END.

www.ingramcontent.com/pod-product-compliance
Lightning Source LLC
Chambersburg PA
CBHW032146160426
43197CB00008B/788